# the Singing Entertainer

## A Contemporary Study of the Art and Business of Being a Professional

### by JOHN DAVIDSON & CORT CASADY

*Library of Congress Cataloging in Publication Data*

*Davidson, John*
*The singing entertainer.*

*Bibliography: p. 227*

*I. Casady, Cort, joint author. II. Title.*

*ISBN 0-88284-095-9*

*Cover Design By Bill Conte*

# CONTENTS

ACKNOWLEDGMENTS      2

ABOUT THE AUTHORS      3

INTRODUCTION      7


Chapter 1   **BEGINNING: THE HUNGRY YEARS**      **13**

Basic Qualities of Singing Entertainers •
Desire, Discipline & Determination •
Growing as a Person • Versatility • Voice
Training • Vocal Coaching • Working With
Other Singers & Musicians • Becoming a
Performer • Using Comedy • Singers' Survey •
Common Pitfalls


Chapter 2   **THE ROLE OF THE SINGING ENTERTAINER**      **31**

The Art of the Singing Entertainer • The
Funk Era • The Glitter Era • The Role of the
Singing Entertainer • Reflecting Musical
Trends • A Commercial Art • The Elements
of Appeal • Mystique • Charisma • Material,
Delivery, Energy, and Rapport • Longevity

*Chapter 3*   **TAILOR-MADE MUSIC**   **57**

Choosing Material • Approaching A Song •
Introduction, Development, Climax, Ending •
Routining a Song • Musical Treatments •
Interpretation • Purpose • Creating A Mood •
Emotional Investment

*Chapter 4*   **PREPARING YOUR ACT**   **79**

Finding Out Who You Are • Individuality •
Buying Material • Medleys • Audience
Participation • Length of Act • Sound •
Lighting • Wardrobe • Make-up • Producer's
Check-List

*Chapter 5*   **"BLAH, BLAH, BLAH"**   **103**

Reasons for Talking On Stage • Your
Opening Talk • Comedy Spots • Setting
Up Songs • Audience Participation • Thank
You's • Good-nights • Censoring Yourself •
Collecting Material • Basic Rules • TV Talk
Shows • Total Communication

*Chapter 6*   **PERFORMING**   **119**

Basic Rules of Performing • Vulnerability •
Pacing • Musical Tricks • Managing The
Audience • Body & Mind On Stage •
Microphone Technique • Types of
Audiences • Intensity vs. Intent • Evaluating
Performances • What To Do If The Show
Isn't Working

*Chapter 7*   **VOCAL STAMINA AND FATIGUE**   **151**

Warming Up • Scheduling Rehearsals
& Shows • Drinking, Smoking & Drugs •
Coping With Vocal Fatigue • Danger
Signals • How To Sing When You Think
You Can't

*Chapter 8*   **RECORDING**      **165**

Demonstration Records • What To Record •
Searching for Songs • Record Producers •
Preparing To Go Into The Studio • Working
In The Studio • Making Copies and
Submitting Tapes • The Art of Recording

*Chapter 9*   **SELLING YOURSELF**      **185**

Becoming Self-Contained Musically • Hiring &
Paying Musicians • Getting Your First Job • TV
Exposure & "Video Demos" • Expanding
Your Base for Jobs • Associating with
Influential People • Press Kits & Promotional
Materials • Agents & Managers • Unions •
Performing Rights Organizations • Promoting
Yourself • Going National • A Team for
Success

*Chapter 10*   **MAKING MONEY**      **211**

Your Gross • Your Net • How To Save
Money • Business Managers & Attorneys •
Contracts

*Chapter 11*   **STRETCHING AS YOU GROW**      **221**

Far-reaching Goals • Dealing With Friends •
Being An Entrepreneur • What To Do About
Reviews • Fear of Success • Pushing
Yourself • Enjoying The Ride

**SUGGESTED READINGS**      **227**

**APPENDIX**      **231**

Sample Questionnaire • Sample Agreement •
Sample Rider Agreement •

# ACKNOWLEDGMENTS

**The authors wish to thank** the following performers who generously contributed their thoughts and suggestions in the course of writing this book: Lynn Anderson, Paul Anka, Hoyt Axton, Pete Barbuti, Pat Boone, Glen Campbell, Harry Chapin, Lola Falana, Bobby Goldsboro, Florence Henderson, Engelbert Humperdinck, Cleo Laine, Janet Lennon, Barry Manilow, Bette Midler, Wayne Newton, Tony Orlando, Freda Payne, Kenny Rogers, Shields & Yarnell, Ray Stevens, Toni Tennille, Jim Teter, Jerry Vale, Andy Williams, and Tammy Wynette.

We also are indebted to newspaper columnist Joe Delaney (*Las Vegas Sun*), television producer Pierre Cossette, arranger Jack Elliott, television director Dwight Hemion, personal managers Jerry Weintraub, Sal Bonafede and Ken Kragen, business manager Hersh Panitch, booking agents Jim Murray and Shannon Green, music publisher Al Gallico, and the students and staff of John Davidson's Singers' Summer Camp (JDSSC).

Additionally, we are grateful for the assistance provided by Dick Lane, entertainment director of the Las Vegas Hilton; Holmes Hendricksen and Doug Bushousen, entertainment directors at Harrah's Hotels in Reno and Lake Tahoe, Nevada; Fred DeCordova, producer of "The Tonight Show;" and Sandy Brokaw, President of the Brokaw Company (public relations).

Finally, a special note of thanks to Cliff Burgess, Billy Fellows, and Nancy Barney, without whose efforts JDSSC and this book would not have become realities.

—John Davidson and Cort Casady

2

# ABOUT THE AUTHORS

**John Davidson began** his show business career in 1963, after graduating with a BA degree in theater arts from Denison University in Granville, Ohio. From Ohio, he went to "The Big Apple"—New York City. There, after struggling for only three months, he was discovered by legendary producer David Merrick and given the juvenile leading role in the Broadway show, "Foxy," starring Bert Lahr. John was 22. (There were to be other theater roles in later years—Curly in the revival of "Oklahoma," for which he received an honor as "Outstanding Newcomer of the Year" from the N.Y. Theater Guild; and starring roles in touring companies of "Carousel," "I Do, I Do," "Music Man," "The Fantastiks," "Camelot" and "110 In The Shade.")

The next person to discover Davidson was TV producer Bob Banner ("The Gary Moore Show," "The Jimmy Dean Show," "Candid Camera" and others). Banner, who had discovered Carol Burnett in "Once Upon A Mattress," saw John in "Foxy" and believed he should become a pop singer. (John was concerned he might become trapped playing juvenile roles on Broadway, so he welcomed the proposal.) In the Fall of 1965, Banner made Davidson a regular on the CBS variety series,

"The Entertainers," and it was on that show that John made his national television debut at the age of 24. The series starred Carol Burnett, Katarina Valente and Bob Newhart, and introduced John Davidson and Dom DeLuise. It ran only one season (26 one-hour shows) but proved to be the beginning of a long, successful relationship with Banner.

In the Spring of 1965, Banner signed Davidson to an exclusive, five year contract and then set about molding John's pop singing career. Banner advised him on what to wear and what to say; he arranged for voice lessons and dance instruction; he groomed him to become a variety television host. John was developed, he says, the way movie studios used to develop new screen stars in the Forties. Finally, after working virtually night and day for several months with Banner, John made his debut as a singing entertainer in mid-1965 at the Elegante supper club in Brooklyn.

In 1966, Davidson hosted his own summer TV series, "The Kraft Summer Music Hall," which launched him as a national star, and secured a long-term recording contract with Columbia Records, for whom he has made eight albums. Also in 1966, he performed for the first time in Las Vegas at Caesar's Palace as opening act for Jack Benny.

In the intervening years, Davidson made records (he later recorded for 20th Century Records), performed in nightclubs and appeared frequently on the David Frost, Merv Griffin and Dick Cavett shows. Then, in 1970, he made his first appearance on "The Tonight Show." With him was his trained, Arabian horse, Poly Royal. Both John and horse were such a hit with Johnny Carson and the audience that John subsequently became a frequent Carson guest. He now is one of a select group of performers who regularly are called upon to guest host "The Tonight Show."

Davidson has made three feature motion pictures—two for Disney ("The Happiest Millionaire" and "The One and Only Genuine Original Family Band") and one for Universal ("Airport '79"). He starred with Sally Field in the 1973 hit NBC comedy series, "The Girl With Something Extra," and he guest-starred in dramatic TV roles on "The F.B.I.", "Owen Marshall, M.D." and, most notably, "The Streets of San

Francisco." He has made two movies for television—"A Time for Love" and "The Mitera Target"—and currently is involved in developing the script for a third.

In addition to other variety TV appearances, since 1976, Davidson has made three Christmas specials with his family (wife Jackie and children John, Jr. and Jennifer), has been a semi-regular guest on "Hollywood Squares," and has hosted such television specials as "John Davidson at Notre Dame," "The Golden Globe Awards" and the "Miss Teenage America Awards."

In recent years, Davidson practically has become an institution in Las Vegas, Reno and Lake Tahoe. After several years of being exclusive to The Riviera, he currently is under contract to the Las Vegas Hilton, where he appears at least nine weeks each year. He also is a long-standing member of the family of performers who work at Harrah's hotels in Lake Tahoe and Reno, Nevada, performing there a minimum of six weeks every year.

**Cort Casady is a songwriter** and performer, in addition to being a television writer and author. A staff writer for Al Gallico Music Corp. (BMI), Casady's songs have been recorded by such artists as Crystal Gayle, Jessi Colter and Marshall Chapman. His variety television credits include writing specials for Kenny Rogers ("A Special Kenny Rogers") and Dan Rowan ("The American Flyer") and a series (75 one-hour shows) for Jim Nabors, on which Cort made his national singing debut in 1978. His dramatic TV credits include stories for such movies as "The Gambler" starring Kenny Rogers, and "Wildfire," based on the songs of the same name.

After graduating from Harvard University in 1968 with an honors degree in political science, Casady worked for the Smothers Brothers, helped produce the Los Angeles production of "Hair" and spent several years as a personal manager of various artists. The product of a newspaper family (his father, Simon Casady, is a retired editor-publisher), he began his writing career doing articles for *San Diego Magazine* and *New West.* Casady, 31, lives in the Hollywood Hills, where he currently is working on his second book, "The Book of Bad Advice."

# INTRODUCTION

**This is** *not* an autobiography or life story.

This is a book for singers.

Moreover, it is a book for singers who strive to do more than just sing. It is a guide for those who want to be entertainers—*singing entertainers.*

A singing entertainer is one who entertains, not only by singing, but also by skillfully employing certain tools and techniques of performing to create a desired effect. A singing entertainer is a student both of the *art of singing* and the *art of entertaining.* A singing entertainer is a dynamic, well-rounded performer who can perform successfully in person, on television, and on records. And a singing entertainer is a contemporary as well as versatile performer who, therefore, is likely to enjoy a long and diverse career.

## JOHN DAVIDSON'S SINGERS' SUMMER CAMP

This book came about because, in the summer of 1978, John Davidson did something which never had been done before—he founded a school which teaches pop singing as an art form and teaches pop singers how to become well-rounded entertainers. The school—John Davidson's Singers' Summer Camp (JDSSC)—has its campus on Catalina Island, 26 miles across the sea from Los Angeles. A non-profit organization, JDSSC primarily is designed to assist young performers between the ages of 18 and 30 who want to become better singing entertainers.

If you are an aspiring singing entertainer, the program offered at JDSSC promises to help in several ways:

1. Save you time and money in the early stages of your career;
2. Expand the scope of your talents and, therefore, your career by introducing you to all styles of popular music;
3. Provide you with a forum for the exchange of contemporary musical ideas by surrounding you with other performers who are striving for the same objectives;
4. Illustrate to you that popular singing, in its most commercial form, is an *art* which has its own rules and formulas and which requires dedication and discipline;
5. Help you make better use of the "tools of the trade" by introducing you to methods for learning how to sight-sing, perform comedy, dance, improve voice production, make records, choose and "routine" (i.e., arrange) songs and put together a well-paced act; and
6. Give you an opportunity to get on-stage experience by performing (at Avalon Bowl) in front of audiences which represent a cross-section of America.

While JDSSC may not be right for every singer, already it has proven to be a remarkably popular idea whose time apparently has come. The first time John mentioned the proposed school on "The Tonight Show," he received some 20,000 inquiries in the mail. Of those initially interested, more than 2,000 turned out to be "serious" applicants who applied for enrollment in the summer of 1978. Because only a limited number of students are accepted in each of the school's month-long sessions, numerous qualified applicants had to be turned away. Again in

1979, the response to JDSSC was overwhelming and enrollment reached capacity several months before the Camp opened. All applicants are subjected to a thorough screening process. (A description of the courses of study, facilities and application procedures for JDSSC follows page 118 of the text.)

John Davidson attends the sessions at JDSSC each summer. He personally gives students critiques of their performances each weekend at the Avalon Bowl; he also lectures and participates in seminars and discussions. As founder, John also uses his considerable influence in Hollywood to attract guest speakers and instructors who come to talk and teach on a wide variety of subjects, from agenting to accounting to songwriting to recording. Among the celebrities who have participated in the past are Kenny Rogers, Florence Henderson, Andy Williams, Shields & Yarnell, Pete Barbuti, TV producer Pierre Cossette and comedian Jim Teter. Among the professionals who teach at JDSSC are experienced booking agents, personal managers, record and TV producers, voice teachers and vocal coaches, musical directors and arrangers, choreographers and musicians.

Incidentally, there is one thing John wants made absolutely clear— the purpose of JDSSC is *not* to turn out a lot of "little John Davidsons." John isn't interested in "cloning" himself. On the contrary, he candidly states that his career has shortcomings as well as strengths. JDSSC is intended to help and encourage those who might wish to further their careers by being aware of the successful techniques of any number of singing entertainers.

## THE PURPOSE OF THIS BOOK

With the creation of JDSSC came the inspiration and need for this book. In fact, most of what is contained in the chapters which follow emerged from an extensive outline John wrote in 1978 to give JDSSC direction and focus at its inception. In those first sessions, John lectured from his outline and used it as a starting point for classes and seminars. Then, in the fall of 1978, taking advantage of the experience he gained by running JDSSC for one summer, he refined the outline further. And in October, he called me to help him write a book which would incorporate not only his concepts and the lessons learned at JDSSC but also basic information about the art and business of becoming a successful singing entertainer.

Hopefully, what we have written is a book which serves three functions. First, it is the "program" or point of view of JDSSC and, as such, a masterplan for courses there. Second, it is a textbook for those who attend JDSSC. And finally, it is a handbook for singers everywhere (especially those who for some reason cannot attend JDSSC) who are interested in becoming better entertainers. Like JDSSC, this book is designed to help you save money in the early stages of your career; encourage you to expand the scope of your talents; give you a better understanding of the business of singing popular music; illustrate how pop singing is an *art* form which has its own rules and formulas and requires dedication and discipline; acquaint you with the "tools of the trade"; and give you insight into the techniques of performing successfully in various media—in person, on television and on records.

This book has been a truly collaborative effort. It is a book neither John nor I could have written separately. Between us, we have had 27 years of experience in various areas of show business and, in every way we could, we have tried to pass along the most important and useful information we have gathered in our vastly different careers. To augment what each of us respectively could bring to the task, we have talked to and interviewed literally dozens of "experts"—people who have "made it" in show business. We sought the advice of successful performers (see acknowledgments), sometimes by interviewing them on video tape and sometimes by sending them a specially-designed questionnaire. We consulted musicians, accountants, choreographers, booking agents, managers, publishers, road managers, attorneys and entertainment buyers. We used transcripts from seminars and discussions in the classrooms at JDSSC; and together we studied the history of pop singing and the careers of those pop singers who have helped define the role of the singing entertainer in America today. For both of us, writing this book was challenging and fulfilling personally as well as professionally. If you, in turn, find it to be enjoyable, informative and thought-provoking reading, we will have achieved our goal.

It is appropriate to mention that, perhaps in testimony to the validity of the basic principles herein, we wrote most of this book in the places where John spends most of his time—on board his yacht, Principia, anchored in Toyon Bay off Catalina; at Interlaken in Reno and Lake Haven on the shore of Lake Tahoe, the sumptuous homes where headliners at Harrah's hotels live; at Poly Royal Farms, John's five-acre ranch in Hidden Hills, California; and "at the end of the rainbow" in the Imperial Suite atop the Las Vegas Hilton.

Cort Casady
Los Angeles, California


All authors royalties from the sale of this book will be donated to John Davidson's Singers' Summer Camp, a non-profit organization.

# CHAPTER 1
# BEGINNING: THE HUNGRY YEARS

*"I miss the hungry years / The once upon a time*
*The lovely long ago / We didn't have a dime*
*Those days of me and you / We lost along the way*
*How could I be so blind / Not to see the door*
*Closing on the world / I now hunger for*
*Looking through my tears / I miss the hungry years."*
*—From "The Hungry Years' by Neil*
*Sedaka and Howard Greenfield ©*
*1974 Don Kirshner Music, Inc.*

**So, you want to be a pop singer?**

Are you sure you don't want to open a shoe store in Columbus, Ohio?

Think about it. You could make a lot of money owning a Mac-Donald's hamburger franchise in your town. Or you probably could get rich selling insurance. One-hour dry cleaning is a good business. There always will be a need for it.

There's supposedly a housing shortage. Shouldn't you consider becoming a building contractor, an architect or an interior designer? Real estate. Now there's a career for you. Your license is your ticket to making millions, they say. And everybody who owns a house is fixing it up—you could make a fortune just remodeling houses!

Why should you become a pop singer?

Consider what's involved. It's a terrible risk. The work isn't steady, at least in the beginning. It's impossible to plan your future. The public is fickle. As a singer, you could be here today and gone tomorrow.

A great percentage of singers are unemployed. Only a handful ever become well-known. Very few are lucky enough to spend much time at the top. And even those who have been extremely successful often end up having little or nothing to show for it when they're no longer "hot."

When you list your occupation as "singer" or "entertainer," you probably will have trouble getting credit. You may not even be able to rent an apartment, much less buy a house, because everyone knows a singer usually has no guarantee of steady employment. You'll have to lie about what you do, or you'll find yourself saying things like, "Right now, I'm a waiter, but I'm really a singer."

So, before you read any further, reconsider opening that shoe store or getting a MacDonald's franchise or going into real estate. But if you're stubborn, if you absolutely have your heart set on a professional singing career, read on. There may be, just *may be,* some hope.


## BASIC QUALITIES OF SINGING ENTERTAINERS

How can you assess whether you have what it takes to become a successful singer? How do you know if you have the basic qualities which will enable you to pursue a singing career?

First, examine your own background. Did you grow up in a musical environment? Did you develop an interest in singing or playing music at an early age? Were you encouraged to be musical? Were you encouraged to be out-going and involved with people? Do you like people? Are you basically a likeable person?

If you answer "yes" to all or most of these questions, you probably already possess one of the most important and commonly-found qualities in successful entertainers.

Every performer is a product, to a large extent, of the events of his childhood. The ability to entertain people is not inherited, it is learned. And, ideally, this learning process should begin at an early age in a supportive environment. Thus, the kind of environment in which you grow up, the age at which you become interested in music, whether you are encouraged to be musical and entertaining—all of these things have a significant and lasting impact on whether you become a performer at all and, if you do, what kind of performer you become.

Growing up in a musical setting and a setting in which you're exposed to people and ideas all the time helps make you a person of greater depth and breadth. Not only do you have music in your life while you're growing up, but also you begin to learn how to extend yourself and function publicly. This is essential early training if you hope to become an effective entertainer.

It is true some singers have become successful on the strength of their voices, their vocal ability alone. When they are not singing, they are shy and introverted; their only means of relating to the audience is through their voice.

But in order to be a versatile, fully-rounded *singing entertainer,* it's essential that you be able to do more than just sing. The singing entertainer must reach out to people, communicate with them in many ways (not only by singing), and *involve* them in an entertainment experience. A singing entertainer must make a commitment not only to moving the vocal chords, but also to moving the listener.

What are the other basic components for a successful career as a singing entertainer?

Talent—vocal, instrumental, writing, acting, dancing—is only *fifty percent* of the equation. The rest is desire, discipline and determination. There are no successful "arm chair" singing entertainers. Singing is not a career for the dilettante. A career as a singing entertainer is so time-consuming and so energy-consuming and so fulfilling that it literally takes over your entire life. Your singing career is something that you work on all the time. Don't sit back and expect it to happen. It won't. You have to make it happen. Particularly when you're starting out, no one will care about your career except you. *You* have to care about it, work on it and worry about it.

In case you haven't heard or read it somewhere else before, there is no such thing as an "over-night success" in the entertainment business. Take any singer you want—Sinatra, Diana Ross, Dylan, John Denver, Toni Tennille or groups like Kiss or The Eagles—they all have one thing in common. They all lived through "the bad old days." They all paid their dues, an average of three to five years of dues, before anything major started to happen in their careers.

Of course, when you hear a song on the radio for the first time and, through that song, meet the singer for the first time, it is natural to assume that the artist has just burst upon the scene. Not true. Whoever spread the word that one could get discovered at Schwab's Drug Store in Hollywood and become a "star" the next day planted false hopes in the hearts and minds of millions of hopeful entertainers.

The singer you hear for the first time on the radio undoubtedly has made dozens of records you never heard, records which did not break through into the public consciousness for one reason or another. And where television is concerned, you can bet that practically everyone who ends up on that little screen in your living room has spent years trying to get there.

## DESIRE, DISCIPLINE & DETERMINATION

What do desire, discipline and determination mean on a day-to-day basis?

They mean you have to want to make it. Every day, regardless of what set-backs you may have experienced the day before, you must tackle your career with new resolve and enthusiasm.

A successful singing career is the result of a steady series of positive, upward moves. Look at your ambition to become an entertainer as a long-term project, one which gives you fulfillment along the way and constantly presents challenges.

Discipline is essential. You must work to improve your natural abilities. You must practice singing constantly.

Practice whatever instrument(s) you play and learn all that you can about music. Learn to play new instruments when you have become reasonably proficient with old ones.

If you're a songwriter, study the accepted forms of popular music and use them. Try to come up with unusual ideas for songs, subjects that commonly are not used. Figure out how to say something that has been said before in a new and interesting way.

While your friends are out drinking beer and going to parties, you should be spending your time either alone or with others who are equally dedicated to musical entertainment. For instance, you could spend your free time doing the following:

Listening to records. This is a good way to find material and learn different styles of singing.

Making lists of different kinds of songs—comedy songs, ballads, uplifting songs, opening and closing songs—which could be used in your show.

Mentally picturing yourself performing for people and thinking about what attitudes or approaches you as a personality will use with the audience. Will you be sexy, dramatic, excited, suave, optimistic, negative, positive, casual, deliberately awkward and so on?

Creating comedy talk spots, ideas for musical segments, concepts for games with the audience or other special material.

Improving your appearance and your physical condition. Your body is your instrument.

Remember you are the creator, the producer, the director, the writer and the choreographer as well as the performer in your career. And there's no end to these jobs.

Don't sit around waiting for someone to hire you. Start working. Structure your time. Set aside certain times to accomplish certain tasks. For example, set aside one day each week for vocal or music lessons. Set aside another day for rehearsals with other musicians or your musical director. Devote one day to practicing singing and/or playing by yourself.

Supporting yourself while you're trying to build your career, even if you're working as an entertainer, is no easy task. One of the most common problems which confronts singers who work in small clubs, restaurants and bars when they're starting out is that they never seem to have time to advance their careers. You work from 9 PM to 2 AM, get to bed by 3 AM, if you're lucky, and get up around noon. After "breakfast," reading the paper, doing a few chores and errands (like dashing to the laundry, the post office or the market), it's time to begin getting ready for work again. There's precious little time left to do the things which might get you better jobs and move your career forward. This is the working entertainer's dilemma. The only solution is to try to organize the time more efficiently when you're not working.

Above all, determination is the key to success in entertainment. Don't be like the singer who came to Hollywood and called his friend to announce that he was in town. The friend asked, "Have you found a place to live, yet?" and the visiting singer replied, "No, I figured I would spend a *week* here and, if nothing happens, I'll go back to Colorado."

Making it requires talent and perseverance in roughly equal proportions. If you think you're the exception to this rule, one day you will have a rude awakening. In the end, you must have some talent so that you can deliver when you finally get the opportunity. On the other hand, even if you have all the talent in the world, chances are no one will ever know it if you don't stay in there pitching. But if you can stay in the game, you might be surprised how well you can do.

Developing your natural talents and polishing your craft can be most rewarding. Some entertainers would even say striving to make it is more exciting and fulfilling than having it made. To borrow the thought from Neil Sedaka, once you've made it, you miss "the hungry years."

The "hungry years" are the time when you prepare or, if you prefer, *program yourself* for success. Perhaps most important of all, you develop as a person and a personality.


## GROWING AS A PERSON

To become a complete singing entertainer, you first must become a complete *person.* As Tony Orlando put it, "Your preparation (for becoming a performer) is your *life.*" What makes a complete person? A number of things help—getting a liberal arts education, being well-informed, meeting interesting people, studying other performers and traveling.

Travel broadens your horizons, makes you more worldly and generally enriches your life. It helps you become a "bigger" person. To use

Tony Orlando's words again, on stage you are "reflecting what has gone on in your life" and pulling from every experience you have had. So, always try to make yourself as "big" a person as possible.

Being well-informed keeps you more contemporary. Not only should you read a major newspaper every day, but also you should read *Time, Newsweek* or *U.S. News and World Report* every week. Read *Rolling Stone,* the best bi-monthly journal of contemporary music and politics in America. Read *Billboard* magazine, the "Bible" of the record business. If you have time, read *Cash Box* and *Record World,* too. Read the trade papers—*Daily Variety* and *Hollywood Reporter.*

Staying abreast of what is happening in your world—the music business—and the world around you only can make you a more complete individual and, therefore, a more well-rounded personality on stage.

Meeting people is also constructive. If you work at becoming an interested person—interested in current events, life styles, trends in music, other people and their careers—you automatically become a more interesting person. If you are both interested and interesting as a person, people will be drawn to you. People will feel like they can relate to you, and you will have better rapport with people on stage as well as off.

Get a liberal arts education, if you can. Lesser degrees, such as a Bachelor of Fine Arts (BFA), are not as valuable. If you're going to college, you might as well settle down and get a Bachelor of Arts (BA) degree in English, music, history, theater arts or one of the sciences. In theory, at least, the BA degree requires that you get a balanced exposure to a variety of important subjects—literature, psychology, mathematics, social studies, languages, art, philosophy, history and so on.

Don't worry about being over-educated for the entertainment business. More people in show business have BA, masters and doctorate degrees than you'd ever imagine. Some make a career out of keeping their education a secret. Kris Kristofferson, for example, successfully played down the fact that he was a Rhodes scholar for the first few years of his songwriting career, apparently because he felt it might confuse the image he was cultivating in country music. But read any of Kristofferson's lyrics and you'll see that there's as much of the Rhodes scholar in his sensitive, expertly crafted imagery as there is the macho, loner, cowboy-poet.

Perhaps the most important thing any degree gives you is confidence in yourself. That confidence, together with a basic higher education, can propel you a long way. And if your singing career doesn't work out, you'll always have that BA (or better) degree. Unfortunately, it is true that a college diploma doesn't guarantee you a job. But it broadens you as a person and, whether you're a singer or not, it gives you a better than average position in the job marketplace.

Studying other performers also is beneficial to your development as a performer. The art of the singing entertainer should be approached the same way you'd approach any other art. If you wish to be a painter, you study the Masters. If you wish to be an architect, you study the great architects. If you wish to become a singing entertainer, study the great singing entertainers from Al Jolson to Barry Manilow, from Bessie Smith to Diana Ross.

Read books. Go to concerts and nightclubs. Watch other singers on television. You can learn, not only from the best, but also from the worst of your contemporaries. Observe the attitudes other performers use when they're singing or telling jokes. Notice the way songs are routined and orchestrated. Be aware of how different performers relate to and communicate with their audiences. As Wayne Newton said in his interview with us, "I've never seen a performer, good or bad, that I didn't learn something from, even if it was what not to do." *Learn what not to do.*

Take a small tape recorder to concerts and nightclubs, record an act, then study it at home. Keep in mind, however, that recording live performances is illegal in most cases. Always ask permission first. Sometimes you will be allowed to make a recording if you can convince the singer and/or his representatives that the tape is for your personal use and study only. Many singers, particularly popular recording artists, do not allow recordings of their live performances to be made under any circumstances. They fear such tapes will be made into so-called "bootleg" or "pirate" recordings over which they will have no quality control and from which they will make no money.

Elvis Presley was a big one for studying other performers. He was notorious for dropping in on shows in Las Vegas. He'd often arrive in town a few days before his engagement was to begin, just so he could go see all the people who were appearing on The Strip. If he came to see you, usually it created considerable excitement.

## VERSATILITY

At the very heart of a successful singing career is one quality we never must neglect—*versatility*. A singing entertainer should be able to work in every medium: nightclubs, concerts, television, recording, film and legitimate theater. The singing entertainer's goal should be to become a *total* variety performer. You should be acquainted with, if not expert at, dancing, acting, comedy, and musical theater, as well as singing. Ultimately, you should be prepared to handle your own variety television show. You should strive to become a performer who is capable of hosting a show and who is equally adept at doing a comedy sketch, telling a joke, delivering a monologue, singing a duet, doing a soft-shoe routine or a dramatic reading.

Even if you're not called upon to use all of these skills at first, you will have them when you need them. And one day, if you're successful, you *will* need them. For example, you will never get an opportunity to host "The Tonight Show" or any other TV show, nor will you be *equipped* to do it, if you don't become a multi-faceted performer.

We cannot over-emphasize the importance of versatility.

## VOICE TRAINING

Obviously, you also must possess some natural vocal ability if you hope to pursue a singing career. And if you have natural talent as a musician and/or as a songwriter, dancer or actor, so much the better.

Let's consider vocal ability and let's assume that you already can sing with some degree of confidence. Now, you may ask, "Should I study voice?" or "Should I go to a vocal coach?" There is a difference. Studying voice and vocal coaching are two different approaches which may be taken to develop and improve natural vocal ability.

*Studying voice* involves learning techniques for singing. The classical approach to voice, the method preferred by most opera and Broadway stage singers, teaches you breathing, breath control, how to sing from your diaphragm, where to place your voice in your head. *Voice training* educates you about the function and use of your vocal chords and, if you have adequate natural ability and pursue the study of voice, eventually you will know how to sing *correctly*. Having studied the technology of singing, you will have greater voice projection, smoother phrasing (due to breathing properly), clearer diction and increased vocal stamina.

However, a surprising number of pop singers have not had voice training. In fact, many singers who have studied voice production tend never to develop a unique vocal sound or distinctive style. Because of their classical orientation, voice teachers seem to try to make all of their students sound the same. But voice training does teach you the basics, and some knowledge of voice production will give you greater stamina and the technical ability to develop your own unique sound. If you choose this route, just keep in mind that the whole purpose of voice traing is to learn technique, *not* style.

Find a voice teacher who is aware of and has an appreciation for contemporary pop singing. A pop singer should learn technique from a pop-oriented voice teacher. When choosing a voice teacher, there are four key things to remember. A good pop voice teacher is one who:

1. Understands microphone technique and will help you increase your vocal range without increasing the size (volume) of your voice;
2. Respects the physical limitations of your voice, particularly in the beginning, and will help you to enhance your vocal ability gradually;

3. Understands and appreciates contemporary pop music and is familiar with various styles, including country, rock, and rhythm and blues; and

4. Encourages you to develop your own natural style and respects your individuality as a singer.

Conversely, you should stay away from voice teachers who:

1. Only teach you how to sing *big,* with volume, and ignore the importance of singing *small* and using a microphone effectively;

2. Abuse your voice by forcing you to do repeated exercises and make you hoarse with overly strenuous lessons. Your voice is to be cared for, nurtured and used correctly. You don't teach it a lesson by kicking it around.

3. Do not appreciate a majority of the successful pop singers in our business, regardless of whether they sing country, rock, pop or rhythm and blues; and

4. Try to interfere with and change the natural sound of your voice or try to make you sing like someone else. Your individuality as a singer is extremely important, and a voice teacher who attempts to take away that individuality is doing you a serious disservice.

The object of voice training is to be able to produce an open sound that flows freely out of you and that sounds like your speaking voice sustained. Some might argue that it is to the pop singer's advantage to forego some of the "correctness" (learned vocal technique) of singing and concentrate instead on feeling and communicating the song. They would say a pop audience does not expect a virtuoso vocal performance from a pop singer. As a matter of fact, the effortless singer who makes perfect tones and vowel sounds is not always revered in pop music. The imperfect voice with minor flaws such as a nasal quality or occasional cracking—in other words, a voice which has rough edges—is attractive and should not be altered. Imperfections in the voice which lend character to it are desirable, so long as they do not cause any permanent damage to the vocal chords.

## VOCAL COACHING

Another way to develop your voice is to work with a *vocal coach.* Although a good vocal coach will know the mechanics of singing correctly, his or her primary function is to help you in approaching specific pieces of material. (A musical director often can serve as an effective vocal coach for the pop singer.)

A vocal coach (or a musical director acting as a vocal coach) should help you choose the songs you sing and then help you to personalize your performance of those songs. Together, you should choose the key in which you will sing each song and work out the routine of each song—verse, chorus, verse, instrumental bridge, chorus, ending, etc. A vocal coach also can assist you by making suggestions about tempos, phrasing and dramatic or comedic interpretation.

Ideally, your vocal coach will know your voice, its strengths and weaknesses, better than anyone else and be able to give you an objective assessment of how you're singing when you lose your perspective. In effect, he or she is a set of ears which hears you the way the audience hears you and, therefore, can help you to better communicate what you are singing. Vocal coaching enables you to define and refine your individual style and maximize your effectiveness as a singer. (We will come back to the subject of approaching pop songs in Chapter Three.)

Incidentally, if you are just beginning to sing, or especially if you've been singing for some time and haven't done this, have your vocal chords examined by a doctor. You should know what your vocal chords look like, what condition they are in, how they function and how to take care of them.

With the advent of optic fibers, your throat doctor probably will be able to let you *see* your own vocal chords in action. A thin tube carrying the optic fiber is inserted through the nose until it reaches the vocal chords (a little topical anesthetic makes this procedure painless). The optic fiber carries a picture of your vocal chords to a small viewer or camera lens, allowing you to see them. If your doctor has the camera, you can have a photograph of your vocal chords. Or you can just sit there and watch them flutter while you say "Ah."

It is also a good idea to have periodic check-ups of your vocal chords to detect early the formation of nodes or rough spots and prevent potentially serious complications. (More about warming up for performances, taking care of your voice and what to do when you lose it in Chapter Seven.)

## WORKING WITH OTHER SINGERS & MUSICIANS

One of the most important people in your singing career will be your musical director. A musical director should be an accomplished musician—pianists usually are preferred—who is familiar with all the various musical styles from jazz to country, classical to disco, rock and blues. Your musical director also should be capable of *writing* as well as playing in a variety of styles and he or she should be able to *conduct* a band or orchestra as well as play in one. Furthermore, a musical director must be someone you trust with your music, for ultimately he or she will be the architect who helps design your act while serving as your best sounding board for musical ideas. And if your musical director also serves as your vocal coach, he or she eventually will be able to give you invaluable insights into your assets and liabilities as a singer and performer.

Working with other singers and musicians also is very beneficial when you are developing as a singing entertainer. Singing in a duo or a group enables you to tune your ear to vocal harmonies and blends. Kenny Rogers (The First Edition), Glen Campbell (The Beach Boys), John Denver (The Chad Mitchell Trio), Diana Ross (The Supremes) and Barry Manilow (conductor and background singer for Bette Midler) are but a few examples of singers who got their start this way.

Remember, though, if you ever hope to stand on your own as a solo performer, don't stay in the background more than two years. Obviously, if you were to become a member of a group like The Eagles, Kiss or Chicago, you'd have a hard time tearing yourself away. As a general rule, however, eventually you must give up the safety, security and comfort of singing with others, as frightening as it might seem, and put yourself out in front as "the star" if stardom is what you seek.

## BECOMING A PERFORMER

Sing at the drop of a hat. When you're starting out, you can't get enough experience. Every opportunity to sing is an opportunity to prove yourself, if not to others, then to yourself. Don't be concerned if you find it difficult to sing for friends and relatives. There's nothing, absolutely nothing, more difficult (and potentially awkward) than performing in your living room for your parents, brothers and sisters and friends. To perform successfully, you must create an illusion; you need to be able to "seduce" your audience. Friends and relatives know you too well, and their proximity to you when you are singing is too close to be able to work any magic on them. Performing for strangers—even thousands of them—is much, much easier.

Get used to the sound of your singing voice. Initially, this is difficult for every singer. The first few times you hear your voice on tape, it doesn't sound like you. Consequently, it's hard to have an accurate perspective on your own performance. But when you have heard your *recorded voice* a few dozen times (more or less), you begin to accept the way you sound. You then can hear a singer—the voice just happens to be yours—singing a song. And when you are able to dissociate yourself from your recorded voice, then you will be able to concentrate on refining each successive performance.

In this age of advanced recording technology and price wars at your local stereo component stores, every singer should be able to afford a reasonably good cassette recorder with a built-in microphone. Until you can afford (or get someone else to pay for) going into a recording studio, record your voice on cassettes. Do it again and again. And after awhile, you probably will hear a singer you really like—you.

## USING COMEDY

An effective entertainer should be able to make people laugh as well as cry or look into themselves. Laughter is fashionable again. In fact, some doctors believe that laughter is vital to good health. It certainly is essential in appealing to most audiences. Laughter breaks down barriers and, especially in the beginning, you need to use humor in order to win acceptance. Explore your potential for comedy. When you think of a joke or make a humorous observation, jot it down in a diary or notebook. (This is also a good way to keep notes about songs you may be writing or musical ideas you wish to pursue.) Don't take yourself too seriously. If you can keep laughing as you go through your career, both the struggle and the final reward will be much sweeter.

## SINGERS' SURVEY

As part of the research for this book, we sent a questionnaire to some of the most prominent singers in America. The questionnaire went to a wide variety of successful pop, country, rock, MOR (middle of the road) and R&B (rhythm and blues) singers. The responses we received are fascinating and yield considerable insight into the beginnings, development and maintenance of successful singing careers. From time to time throughout the book, we will refer to the results of this survey.

In terms of what we have discussed thus far—that is, what it initially takes to become a singing entertainer—the survey sheds light on several key points:

First: ninety-nine per cent (99%) of those responding said music was a part of their upbringing.

Second: 3 out of 5 said there were other musical people in their family.

Third: 4 out of 5 of those responding described themselves as "basically shy" people.

Fourth: 3 out of 5 singers said they read a daily newspaper at least once a week and a selection of news and music trade magazines.

Fifth: The *average* age for starting a singing career was 19; the *average* age when the singer first felt he had attained some success was usually three years later, at 22.

Sixth: Only 1 out of 5 singers responding said they had studied voice, but that appears to relate to the next finding.

Seventh: 3 out of 5 said "personality" was the quality which contributed most to their success. (Barry Manilow said "personality" and "professionalism" were both more important than "vocal ability" in his case. Pat Boone put "personality" first, "vocal ability" second and "appearance" third.)

Finally: 3 out of 5 singers said they had worked in a duo or vocal group; the average length of time was four years.

(A sample of the questionnaire sent to singers is included in the Appendix.)

## COMMON PITFALLS

If you've read this far, you probably already have a reasonably good idea of what it takes to begin your career as a singing entertainer. The basic ingredients are: having music in your background, preferrably at an early age; having some natural vocal talent, hopefully combined with the ability to play a musical instrument or two and/or write songs; and having the desire, discipline and determination to succeed.

To get started, you need to: develop as a well-rounded person; make yourself a versatile performer; strive to improve your natural talents; work with a musical director, other musicians and singers; study other performers; and perform every chance you get.

And when you're starting out, you should avoid, if possible, these common pitfalls:

1. Don't quit your day job until you are reasonably sure you can survive by singing for a living.
2. Don't begin a singing career much later than age 25.
3. Don't be concerned if you feel more inhibited when performing for friends. Strangers are easier.
4. Don't pattern yourself too closely after someone else. Imitation, at times, is okay, but impersonation is a dead-end street.
5. Don't assume you have to be loud, outspoken and always "on" to be a success in show business.
6. Don't sing with a vocal group for more than two years with no chance as a soloist.
7. Don't remain a background singer for other artists or on records for more than two years unless you have an opportunity to become a soloist.
8. Don't remain a chorus singer in stage shows for more than two years unless you have an opportunity to become a soloist.
9. Don't expect to be an over-night success; it takes an average of three years before your singing career will begin to pay off, often longer.
10. Don't give up. If you know what you want and apply yourself (persist!), eventually your number will come up.

# CHAPTER 2

# THE ROLE OF THE SINGING ENTERTAINER

*"Let me sing a funny song*
*With crazy words that roll along*
*And if my song can start you laughing*
*I'm happy, I'm happy."*
*—"Let Me Sing-And I'm Happy"*
*by Irving Berlin. © 1929-1955*
*Irving Berlin, Used with permission.*

**To study any art form,** you must study those who have excelled at or mastered the art.

A man named Al Jolson was the first bona fide singing entertainer and, for a long time, the greatest. He was a pioneer of the art.

At the turn of the century, Jolson was the first to achieve major success as a singer of popular music and, thus, helped establish popular singing as we have come to know it as a commercially viable form of entertainment.

Before Jolson, popular music in America and throughout most of the world was identified with a European musical idiom—so-called "serious" or Classical music. It was sung by classically-trained opera, oratorio and concert singers.

By the beginning of the 19th Century in America, however, popular music had begun absorbing and reflecting the influences of another musical idiom—Afro-American. And by the beginning of the 20th Century, the music of Black America, not the classical music of Europe, was a revolutionary force in popular music.

The influence first was seen when blacks began imitating or parodying the manners and speech of their white masters. Whites found this so amusing and charming that they, in turn, parodied the imitation for their own amusement. Hence, the tradition of the minstrel show was born. Whites blacked their faces to imitate blacks imitating whites. Then blacks followed suit in their own minstrel shows, blacking their already black faces to imitate whites imitating blacks.

By the time Al Jolson and Sophie Tucker came along, popular music in America had its roots planted deeply in black American music, whose African heritage also gave us the blues, ragtime, jazz, gospel song, and rhythm-and-blues (R&B or soul.) But it was through the songs and singing of Jolson and Tucker that pop music was truly revolutionized.

Jolson started out singing what were then called "coon songs," often wearing blackface and appearing in a minstrel show type of presentation. With the success of such songs as "My Mammy" and "Take Me To That Swannee Shore," Jolson popularized what was essentially Afro-American music. Later, thanks to Jolson, these songs became known as "mammy songs" (which still seems offensive by today's standards) or simply "blues" songs. They were written by both black and white songwriters and sung by both black and white singers.

## THE ART OF THE SINGING ENTERTAINER

There's an old saying that "Art is that which disguises art." In this sense, Al Jolson exemplified the *art* of popular singing. Whereas with classical singers, the art of singing often had been all too obvious, Jolson made it seem easy, effortless. Because of the Afro-American music idiom, he was able to take liberties which the classical singer could not. In his interpretation of songs—his shading, phrasing, rhythm, enunciation and accentuation—Jolson set an example which popular singers have followed basically ever since.

Through the strength of his own personality and his zest for performing, Jolson made it popular for a singer to be a showman, a powerful on-stage personality. He defied tradition and commonly accepted ideas

AL JOLSON IN BLACK FACE            AL JOLSON

SOPHIE TUCKER (supplied by World Wide Photos)

33

about what constituted "good stage manners." He insisted on being an individual, both in his approach to songs and to audiences. And it was Jolson who was the first to successfully challenge and break down the invisible barrier which traditionally had existed between the singer and the audience.

Remember the Gardol shield from the old Colgate toothpaste commercials? It was the invisible shield which the toothpaste theoretically created to protect your teeth from decay. That's the kind of barrier there was between singers and audiences until Jolson came along. He kicked a hole in that shield and stepped right through.

In about 1913, Jolson caused a sensation in show business by jumping into theater aisles to sing his songs intimately to the people. This was unheard of at the time. (Actually, according to Abel Green and Joe Laurie in *Show Biz: From Vaude to Video,* Burlesque singer Dave Marion was the first to pull such an antic in 1912.) Before Jolson, singers stayed center stage, well behind the footlights. There was an unwritten law or at least tradition that said the singer should not invade the audience's territory. That would be rude.

But Jolson broke the rules. First, by singing black music and, second, by refusing to accept any limitations on his freedom as a performer. The result was people flocked to see him. In 1913, he started working for the Shuberts (the prominent theatrical entrepreneurs) in New York for $250 a week; by 1920, he was earning $2,000 a week and the Shuberts had named a theater for him. Jolson's popularity grew by such leaps and bounds that, by 1927, he was earning $17,000 a week, plus a percentage of the gross, at the L.A. Metropolitan theater. Two years later, in San Francisco's Warfield Theater, he smashed all house records, earning a $57,000 gross. That was a lot of money in 1929 when the dollar was worth a dollar.

The most important thing about Jolson, however, is that he set an example for other singers to follow. He was a role model. He loved the audience, any audience, so long as it physically was there for him to entertain. Every new audience and every show presented a new challenge, another opportunity for conquest.

Jolson insisted on being familiar with his audience, which also was considered brash at the time. He would go into the audience; he would stand in the footlight trough and talk to the audience. Sometimes, he would call to the stage crew, "Bring up the house lights!" Then, he'd go sit down on the edge of the stage, loosen his collar, take off his tie and proceed to hold people spell-bound with songs and patter. (In case you were wondering, Tom Jones did not invent the idea of taking off your tie on-stage.)

Jolson couldn't stand to let an audience go, either. Always one to give audiences more than their money's worth, he once held a Chicago audience after the show to hear him rehearse a new song. (It was George Gershwin's, "Who Cares?") Often, he refused to sing the same songs in every show, thus audiences would stay to hear new songs in his second show. The box office suffered when he did this, but it was Jolson's way of putting his audience first.

"The King," Al Jolson, died in 1950, leaving an estate valued at $4 million. There were huge crowds at his memorial services in New York City and Hollywood. Eddie Cantor, who delivered the eulogy in New York, was quoted as saying, "Jolson turned them away again."

The role of the singing entertainer has not changed very much over the years. After Jolson and Tucker, Eddie Cantor, Bessie Smith, Ethel Waters, Louis Armstrong and a lot of others perpetuated and improved upon what Jolson started. He broke the ground, and those who followed tilled it.

(Eddie Cantor was the first to capitalize on the precedents which Jolson had set. For example, whereas the Old Gold cigarette company had paid Jolson an unheard of $2,500 to endorse their smokes, they now paid Cantor $7,500 for his signature. Imagine, singers endorsing cigarettes!)

Nowadays, obviously, it is neither revolutionary nor controversial to be a popular singer who interacts with the audience. Popular singers are in the mainstream of American music. We have watched the likes of Judy Garland, Frank Sinatra, Bobby Darin, Sammy Davis, Jr., Tony Orlando, Wayne Newton and Diana Ross further define and extend the role of the singing entertainer. We have seen popular singing become an enormous business.

And then there's Las Vegas.

Las Vegas is the mecca of popular singing entertainers. Except for the advent of the microphone and recording, Las Vegas probably has done more to keep alive and encourage the growth of what Al Jolson started. In Las Vegas, Reno, Lake Tahoe and now, Atlantic City, the singing entertainer is king. He or she is as important to the gambling business in each of these cities as the chips, the tables or the dice.

The role of the singer as an entertainer has never been more important than it is in the late 1970s. And it appears the trend will extend well into the 1980s, perhaps even through the end of the 20th Century. However long it lasts, it is undeniable that in the last few years there has been a remarkable return to entertainment as an art form. The *show* is the thing.


**THE FUNK ERA**

In the late 1960s and early 1970s, however, this was not the case. Largely due to the climate created by the war in Vietnam, America entered The Funk Era. It wasn't fashionable to entertain—not the way it is now or had been at other times. The Funk Era was a period in which hard-rock music dominated the American music scene and hard-rock performers displayed, if anything, an anti-entertainment attitude. Some rock performers gave entire performances with their backs to the audience. Instead of dressing up for a show—a custom which dates back centuries—performers wore whatever they had on at the moment or, in some cases, even dressed *down.* The question at the time was, "How funky can you be?" It was a time when we had music blasted at us; and it was an era in which anything slick or polished—as well as anything humorous—was not fashionable. Perhaps the only place where entertaining the old way survived was Las Vegas.

Bill Medley, one-half of the legendary recording group, The Righteous Brothers, remembers the period from about 1969 to 1973 as being "a depressing hunk of history," as many performers undoubtedly do. It was difficult to entertain during The Funk Era the way we think of entertaining today. Singers who simply tried to make people happy and provide them with an escape from everyday problems were viewed as irrelevant. If you didn't reflect the anger, protest and rebellion which was so prevalent in the country, you were labeled a member of "the establishment." They used to say, "If you're not part of the solution, you're part of the problem."

In retrospect, it seems that, until the Vietnam war ended finally in 1973, people either didn't want to have or were incapable of having a good time. It was a serious time, a time when our country was wrestling with gut-wrenching problems. And entertainment for the sake of entertainment was an indulgence we couldn't seem to afford.

Entering the 1980s, however, America once again is experiencing lighthearted fun, even frivolous entertainment. It may be escapist entertainment. Certainly, all our problems haven't vanished but at least now, people are willing and able to escape.

As we approach the '80s, the country literally is laughing, dancing, jogging and dressing up again. We have entered The Glitter Era.


## THE GLITTER ERA

Beginning with Elton John in the mid-'70s and continuing with such performers as Barry Manilow, Billy Joel, Donna Summers, John Denver and others, we have seen a resurgence in the importance of becoming an exciting performer, having a positive attitude on stage and an optimistic outlook on life in general.

Whereas The Funk Era was characterized by the use of psychedelic drugs, ultra-long hair and hard-rock music, The Glitter Era, thus far at least, has been typified by a return to drinking alcohol, wearing shorter hair and listening to more melodic music.

During The Funk Era, it wasn't "hip" to dress up—unless you call wearing blue jeans with patches all over them dressing up. But in The Glitter Era, if you don't look sharp, you aren't chic. If there's a motto for the late '70s, it's "Have a good time"—a good time disco roller skating, disco ice skating, disco dancing or going to movies or to concerts where the performer offers something more than music—a show.

In October, 1978, *The Hollywood Reporter* published the results of a survey by the Newspaper Advertising Bureau which asked people why they go to movies and what kind of movies they like. The results suggest a mood which we believe is prevalent in America among all types of audiences, whether they are going to see movies, musical groups or singing entertainers.

Two-thirds of those quizzed said that going to the movies was "a great way to get out of the house." 37% said they went to movies "to laugh and be happy," while only 11% said they went "to improve myself and think." Given a choice between a thought-provoking film and one that lets you forget your problems, 56% chose the *escapist* movie.

So, if you want to become a singing entertainer, you probably couldn't pick a better time than right now. The role of the singing entertainer in show business never has been more significant.


## THE ROLE OF THE SINGING ENTERTAINER

Let's look at what it means to be a contemporary popular singing entertainer. What is our role?

You should see yourself for what you are—*hired entertainment.* Some critics even may go so far as to say you are a prostitute. Like those who practice the world's oldest profession, you are paid to please. But this is an unduly harsh analogy. A singing entertainer also is an artist who moves you with his music. Still, as an entertainer, you are part of a time-honored tradition of being paid to perform. And more often than not, the object of performing is to make people happy and give them enjoyment.

Moreover, it feels good to make others happy. There's joy in pleasing people. That's why you do what you do—it's not only the money.

You have to love your audience. That's what Jolson did so well. At the end of a song, he would say, "You ain't heard nothin' yet!" He was saying, in effect, "I want to give you more" and "I hope this moment never ends." That's how you should feel when you're in front of an audience.

You also should make the audience feel important. As a performer, you are put on a pedestal. The audience, literally as well as figuratively, looks up to you. You are larger than life to them. The trick is to accept this role and use it but, at the same time, not be intimidating or aloof. By letting your audience see that you have the same problems they have and by being able to laugh at yourself, you make them feel bigger. If you allow some of your vulnerability to show—especially your love for the audience—the audience will embrace you as you embrace them.

It may be that loving to be an entertainer requires that you *need* to be an entertainer. Perhaps the reason we sing for people is that we need the love and attention they give us back. To whatever extent this is true, it's not necessarily bad. The give-and-take is healthy.

## REFLECTING MUSICAL TRENDS

A singing entertainer is a mirror for his audience. You must reflect both the times in which you are singing and the people who are listening. You must allow the audience to enjoy themselves and escape from their own lives through what you do. As a mirror for your audience, it also is possible to show them something about their own lives and human relationships through the songs you sing.

Al Jolson was a trend-setter in that he popularized a new style of music and made famous a number of songs. You should strive to do the same. However, in the early stages of your career, you also must be aware of currently popular trends in music.

Being aware of popular musical trends makes you a better mirror for your audience. If disco is the rage  which it is as this is being written— then you should include disco songs in your act. If music from the '50s is the thing, which it was a few years ago, your repertoire should include a '50s nostalgia routine. While you are developing your unique musical identity, you never can go wrong by staying up to date with whatever style, mood or fashion currently is popular in music.

A singing entertainer should sing *public songs,* in other words, songs which not only have been major hit records, but also which appeal to and have reached the broadest possible audience. Public songs are songs you would expect to become so-called "standards." Mac Davis' "I Believe In Music" is a public song. "I Write the Songs (That Make the Whole World Sing)," a hit for Barry Manilow, is a public song. "Tie A Yellow Ribbon (Around the Old Oak Tree)" was a public song. When "Yellow Ribbon" was a hit for Tony Orlando and the record was high on the music charts, it was being sung by singing entertainers. More importantly, it was a song *people* were singing. All kinds of people— young record buyers, their parents, grandmothers and grandfathers— were familiar with it.

Not all songs that are hit records become public songs. When you are choosing material for your act (see Chapter Three), try to determine whether songs that currently are popular on the radio and among record buyers also are familiar to the broader audience. Have they reached the masses?

## A COMMERCIAL ART

The art of the singing entertainer is a commercial art form and you've got to find out what will make you a saleable product. What will interest people? What will make people *care* about you? What will make people pay to see you or buy your records or turn on their television sets to watch you?

A performer becomes interesting to an audience when that performer makes the audience feel like they are important and they are included. The singer sings well-known songs because it is flattering to the audience. Familiar material makes them feel knowledgeable, "hip." It's *in*clusive, not *ex*clusive. Likewise, comedy material that depicts the universality of our experiences is flattering to the audience because they can identify with it. You must take the edge off your elevated place on stage by using self-effacing humor and by showing the audience that you feel the same things they feel.

You are the product. Always keep that in mind. And, as a product, you need to be packaged and sold. This should not be done in a gimmicky way. You don't want to end up like "Pet Rocks," a fad one day and forgotten the next. You want to be a product you can sell your whole life long. And, if you're successful, you'll be able to afford to pursue your career for as long as you want.

Always remember that, by definition, a singing entertainer is a commercial commodity. You are part of a business in which profits are as important as artistic achievement. If this scares you, or if you think you're too good, too pure or artistic, too special or delicate to be a commercially viable entertainer, then you should get out of the business. You'd be better off never taking your music to town.

In show business (and remember, it is a *business*), commercial success is the key to artistic freedom. You should seek commercial acceptance because it will give you the power to choose the jobs you want, the people you want to work with, and the ultimate direction of your career. Commercial strength actually gives you artistic strength; it paves the way for you to do what you want, when you want—and get paid for doing it.

So, the role of the singing entertainer is based on commercial acceptance. You're hired entertainment. You have to love your audience and please them. You're a mirror for the audience; through you, they must be able to experience themselves and, from you, they must get public songs and comedy which enables them to feel included, and important.


## THE ELEMENTS OF APPEAL

You may be thinking, "All I want is to be able to perform and make a lot of money." You want audiences to want you. You want there to be demand for your product. You want to develop *audience appeal.*

What, then, constitutes the thing we call appeal in a performer? What elements go into making a performer attractive to an audience? What combination of things enables a singer to draw people in to watch, listen and be a part of what he or she does?

Appeal is a very individualistic quality. A variety of factors are involved in attracting an audience to what you do and in getting a favorable response from that audience.

First, there are two personal qualities—charisma and mystique. They comprise the "X" factor, the unknown variable among performers. Some performers possess these qualities, some don't. Certainly, some singers have more charisma and/or mystique than others.

## MYSTIQUE

In terms of mystique, it's useful to understand that people usually perceive performers to be in one of two categories. A performer is either regarded as "approachable" or "unapproachable." As a general rule, those who are thought of as approachable have less mystique. That is, there are fewer mystical beliefs and attitudes held about them. They are perceived to be (whether they are or not) more accessible, more open and more ordinary. Performers who are thought of as unapproachable are perceived to be less open, less accessible and, therefore, more unusual. Their lives and their work give rise to mystical beliefs and attitudes. And even though they may be very public people and highly visible, they nevertheless seem distant, almost unreachable.

When a performer is perceived to be unapproachable, inevitably he is surrounded by an air of mystery—people want to know what he really is like and how he lives.

Elvis Presley, most of his life, seemingly was unapproachable. He had great mystique. Was he a prisoner of his own stardom? What did he do when he was alone? Whom did he love? Who really loved him? Conjecture about Elvis' off-stage life—the life of a man we could not know or see, except when he was performing—filled fan magazines for two decades. And speculation about Elvis continues even after his death. That's mystique.

Bob Dylan has enormous mystique. For years, his career has been shrouded with mystery. He is private, even reclusive. He won't do interviews (neither would Elvis). He is remote and reluctant to show us anything of himself which isn't expressed in his songs. Thus, the mystical beliefs and attitudes which surround Dylan never have been dispelled. Rather, they have grown.

The Beatles are another example of pop singers who had (and still have) mystique. Their lives were the subject of rumors and intriguing theories. For a long time, John, Paul, George and Ringo appeared to be so unapproachable, and so little was known about them as individuals, that they were a tantalizing mystery.

And mystery breeds mystery.


## CHARISMA

Charisma is a different quality, though equally important. It is also more common among entertainers and, in a sense, more basic. Charisma is the special magnetic charm or appeal which a person has which inspires others to be enthusiastic and loyal in their support for that person. Some argue that charisma is God-given. Others maintain that charisma can be developed. Probably, both are correct. Children often are naturally charismatic; however, as they get older, they become more inhibited and, hence, more afraid of using whatever natural magnetism they may have.

Truly charismatic people usually are aware that they possess this quality. And, to some extent, they do things to nurture the traits which make them charismatic. If mystery breeds mystery, then exploring your own potential to be charismatic only can make you more charismatic.

Most successful, contemporary singing entertainers are charismatic. While they may not be surrounded by mystique, they possess the equally alluring qualities of openness, honesty and vulnerability. Still,

Frank Sinatra

*Which of the performers pictured on the next 4 pages have mystique? Which have charisma?*

Olivia Newton-John

Linda Ronstadt

eil Diamond

Barbra Streisand

Elvis Presley

Barry Manilow

Lola Falana

Judy Garland

Dolly Parton

Tony Orlando

John Denver

Sammy Davis, Jr.

Ben Vereen

Englebert Humperdinck

charisma is a difficult quality to define. Being a charismatic performer starts with believing you are a winner, believing you are attractive (whether or not you are handsome or pretty), believing you have the ability to affect other people, and believing you have something to offer others. And charisma develops as you develop as a person, a personality and a performer. Observe charisma in others and be aware of having it yourself. For charisma is unquestionably one of the most important variable factors in becoming an appealing performer.

Also, you may wish to make a conscious decision at some point in your career as to whether you wish to be an approachable or unapproachable performer. This is not an easy choice to make. To some extent, it simply has to evolve. But if you feel that being approachable is what suits you best and what comes most naturally, go with that. Don't fight it. And don't try to manufacture an air of mystery about yourself. That would be contrived. There's nothing wrong with being an open, accessible type of personality.

## MATERIAL, DELIVERY, ENERGY & RAPPORT

The other elements which make a performer appealing and insure a favorable response from an audience are easier to deal with and are more tangible. They are elements you can experiment with and, to a large extent, control.

They are: (1) Material—the songs you sing; (2) Delivery—the *way* you sing; (3) Energy—the commitment you make to your total performance; and (4) Rapport—your unique relationship with your audience. Although they may be combined in differing quantities by different performers, when taken together, they add up to a performance which gets a favorable response.

This method of looking at what makes a performer appealing came about by asking the question: "How can a John Denver, a Rod Stewart, an Ann-Margaret and a Linda Ronstadt be successful in the same business?" They are so different. Except for their love of music, they would appear to have practically nothing in common in terms of the way they approach performing. Yet, when they perform, each gets a favorable response from their audience. Some combination of basic elements must exist in their performances, though surely in differing amounts.

What all performers have in common is one very significant thing. They all determine the success or failure of their respective performances by the way in which they combine these four basic elements of appeal—Material, Delivery, Energy and Rapport. Whether they are conscious of it or not, an Engelbert Humperdinck, a Donna Summers, a Roy Clark and a Tanya Tucker all rely on the marriage of these elements in their performances to achieve a successful end result.

Take Linda Ronstadt, for example. Basically, her Material is her hits. She can do at least ten songs in her act which she has made famous. It's remarkable. If she did nothing more than walk on stage and vocally duplicate her hits ("Heat Wave," "Long, Long Time," "You're No Good," "Silver Thread and Golden Needles," "Love Has No Pride," "Different Drum," etc.), she'd get a fine reaction from the audience.

Let's say, therefore, that Material in Linda Ronstadt's performance accounts for at least 50% of the response she gets. People love to hear those songs. But Ronstadt also is a gifted pop singer, known not only for what she sings but *how well* she sings. Hence, her Delivery is also a crucial element in the success of a performance. If Linda does a concert-type performance with reasonably good pacing, her commitment as a performer—Energy—further contributes to her appeal. And the fourth element, Rapport, adds to the response she gets. When you analyze any artist in this way, you can begin to get a picture of what elements are most important to that artist in terms of appealing to an audience. After seeing Linda in concert, draw your own conclusion as to how these four elements contribute to her success.

The survey of singers conducted for this book sheds some light on how those surveyed viewed the importance of Material, Delivery, Energy and Rapport in their respective cases.

Barry Manilow, who has numerous hit records to his credit, said that his Rapport with the audience accounts for 70% of the reaction he gets. He said Material accounts for 10%; Delivery accounts for 10%; and Energy accounts for 10%.

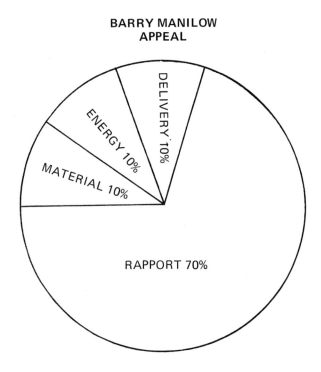

**BARRY MANILOW APPEAL**

It is true that Manilow has a special rapport with his audience. He is viewed as a romantic figure, poetic and vulnerable, though his songs are elaborately produced and staged; and he believes in having a good time, mixing comedic moments with dramatic ones.

However, a typical audience might see Manilow's appeal differently. The mixture of elements would be more evenly distributed. For instance, most people who buy his records do so (a) because they like his songs and (b) because they like his voice. Hence, these same people would go to a Barry Manilow concert with high expectations as to his Material and Delivery. In their view, his appeal might be seen as follows:

**BARRY MANILOW**
**APPEAL FROM AUDIENCE'S**
**POINT OF VIEW**

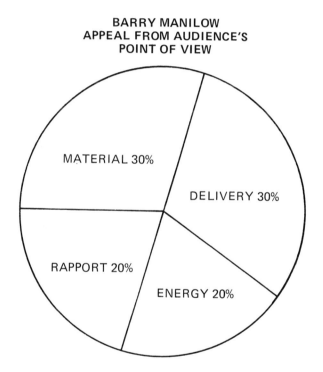

Which simply suggests that a singer may see his appeal in one way, and his audience may see it in another. Thus, as a performer, you must ask yourself what makes you appealing; then you must ask *other people* to tell you how they see you. The truth lies somewhere in between.

Jerry Vale assessed his appeal to audiences as follows:

**JERRY VALE APPEAL**

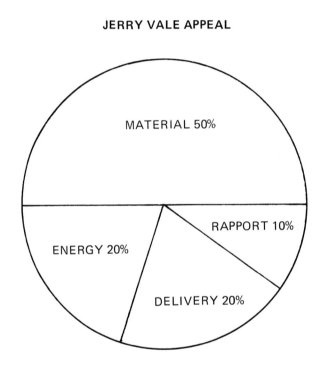

Pat Boone, like Manilow, said much of his appeal depends on his Rapport with the audience—50%. Delivery was next—30%. Choice of Material and Energy were each 10%.

PAT BOONE APPEAL

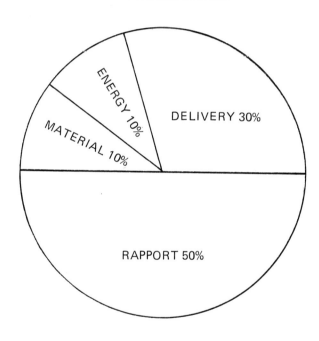

Ray Stevens said his appeal was based on an equal mixture of the four basic elements.

**RAY STEVENS APPEAL**

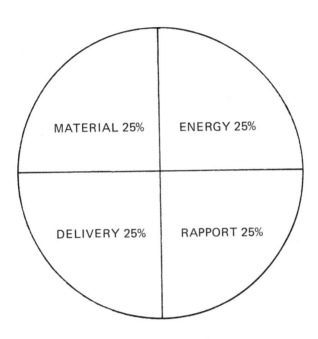

MATERIAL 25%     ENERGY 25%

DELIVERY 25%     RAPPORT 25%

In a seminar at JDSSC, John Davidson described his appeal to audiences this way: "I tend to mix the elements of appeal—Material, Delivery, Energy and Rapport—in roughly equal proportions. If there is one element which is more important, it is *Rapport.* My relationship with my audience has become an essential element in getting a consistently good response. Also, when I go on-stage, I try to make a maximum commitment to each performance and keep the energy up. So, at least in front of audiences, the Energy element is very important to me."

**JOHN DAVIDSON APPEAL**

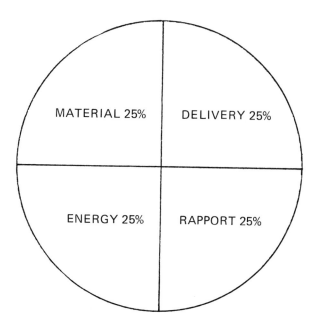

## LONGEVITY

If you have come this far, hopefully you now have a better fix on the role of the singing entertainer in show business. And perhaps you now have a better understanding of what personal qualities and elements of performing make an entertainer appealing.

Keep in mind as you read on that a singing entertainer is not merely one who sings. A singing entertainer is *more* than a singer. You must be capable of grabbing an audience and holding them in a spell for an entire performance. You must take the audience on a well-planned journey, a journey on which the ride must be as enjoyable and fulfilling as arriving at the destination. You must *wear* your music like a tailor-made suit. Whereas the classical singer stands back from the music, you, the popular singer, must step forward and embrace it. If the song fits, wear it.

The singing entertainer uses many tools—comedy, conversational "patter," audience participation, medleys (musical compositions made up of various songs or short musical pieces), choreography and other devices for pacing—which we will discuss later. Whatever your tools, you must love to perform and love your audience. You must see every performance as a challenge and win every audience with love.

We have mentioned the names of some singers who have built their careers on hit records. There's no question that a hit record is one of the most effective and fastest ways to launch a successful singing career. But one hit is not enough. It takes an average of *three* Top Ten records (on the national charts) to establish a singer as a major attraction, in other words to make you a "star."

If, while you are working to get your first hit record and two more hits to follow that, you also work at becoming a versatile entertainer, your career will continue to prosper. You may not have a meteoric rise to fame, but you will enjoy a gradual ascent. When you know how to entertain, you don't have to be "hot" all the time. Your career will warm up steadily over the years.

On the contrary, if you're a singer whose career rises or falls with your latest hit record (or TV series), then you will be doomed to ride what Kenny Rogers has called "The Music Business Roller Coaster" through its many tortuous ups and downs.

Become a well-rounded performer and you will have a singing career of life-long proportions.

CHAPTER 3

# TAILOR-MADE MUSIC

*"The woods would be very silent if no birds sang except those that sang the best."*
*—Thoreau*

**Picture yourself in a record store** a supermarket of records. Before you is a massive collection of musical choices. As you survey the aisles, there are records of every style and description—jazz, opera, rock, classical, rhythm and blues (soul), Broadway shows, religious, disco, country and pop. You're looking at thousands upon thousands of songs.

Stop! Before you get hopelessly lost in this sea of musical choices, take time to chart yourself a course.

You need material. But how should you go about choosing it? What criteria should you use for choosing the songs you are going to sing? Where do you start?

You may pass by the bins filled with opera, classical and jazz records. You're looking for contemporary pop music. Browse for a moment in the "Broadway shows" section. But keep in mind that very few songs from Broadway shows are well-known enough or universal enough in their appeal to be included in your act. There always will be a few possibilities—Broadway songs like "I Don't Know How To Love Him" from "Jesus Christ Superstar" or, more recently, "What I Did For

Love" from "Chorus Line" or "Tomorrow" from "Annie." But generally, Broadway songs appeal to a relatively small, elite, sophisticated audience.

You also can pass by the religious records. Religious songs, while they are inspirational and enjoyable to sing, appeal to a select and comparatively limited audience. And if you sing religious songs, you immediately become typed as a religious singer. You might want to find an uplifting gospel song which doesn't have a specifically religious lyric. But often these songs, if they truly have broad appeal, will be found on pop, country or soul records as well.

Keep moving.

A singing entertainer sings the contemporary pop songs of our time. So, move on to the sections which contain pop, rock, country and soul records. Now you're in the right area. But you still are faced with a crisis of too many choices. There are hundreds of contemporary pop, country and soul songs from which to choose. On what basis should you select songs which might possibly go into your act?

## CHOOSING MATERIAL

There are three basic rules:

First, you must *identify with the songs you sing.* Consider songs which say something to you, songs which reach you in some way and which embody a thought, a message or a sentiment you would like to share with an audience.

Once you have found such a song, ask yourself if you can sing it? Is the song suited to your vocal ability? Technically, can you sing it comfortably? If you can sing the song, ask yourself if you would *enjoy* singing it. Once you include a song in your act, you're going to be singing it over and over again. Thus, it should be a song you won't tire of quickly. Now ask yourself if you would be believable singing the song. You may be able to sing it technically, and you may enjoy singing it. But can you sing the song convincingly?

Second, *the song must appeal to a broad audience.* Ask yourself if the song has universal appeal. Does it embody some universal truth? Is the lyric one with which the general public, young and old, can identify? Will the song touch or speak to the average person in some way?

By applying these two criteria, you can eliminate a tremendous number of songs. But once you have a song with which you can identify and which will appeal to a broad audience, you still have to observe one more rule.

The third rule is most of your songs *must be familiar.*

Ask yourself if the song you've chosen is a "public song," in other words a song which has become a part of the public's consciousness. If you're not sure whether a song is well-known enough, ask a clerk at the record store how well the record has sold. Consult the music trade papers, particularly *Billboard* magazine's lists of the "Hot 100" albums and singles for that week.

Before you go to the record store, listen to Top 40 radio to get an idea of what songs are being played most frequently. Be aware of the fact that it takes about 4 to 6 months for a hit record to become a "public song." A song that has been in the Top 40 for only a few weeks may not yet have reached the status of being a universally accepted hit song.

Listen to contemporary Middle of the Road (MOR) stations which play so-called "easy listening" music. Check their playlists. Songs which are being played on Top 40 stations, soul stations, country stations and MOR (Easy Listening) stations are known as "across-the-board" hits and are likely to become universally-known songs.

Go see movies. More and more, movies are launching pads for pop songs and musical trends. For example, "Saturday Night Fever" established the disco trend. "You Light Up My Life" came out of the motion picture by the same name.

Television is another barometer of public taste. The TV networks are ruthless. If a musical trend isn't popular with the mass audience, television usually won't touch it. Watch television variety shows and talk shows (especially "The Tonight Show") to see what currently popular songs are being sung. This is usually a good indication of whether a song has become or is about to become a "public song."

Be certain, if you can, that a song has reached the nonrecord-buying public. According to an interview with Warner Bros. Records executive Stan Cornyn in *Rolling Stone* (November 30, 1978), the greatest body of American record buyers is in the twenty-five to thirty-four age bracket. But concert and nightclub audiences are comprised of people in their Teens as well as people in their Forties and Fifties. You want songs that speak to all audiences.

Remember that familiar material is essential because it flatters your audience. Familiar songs make the listener feel included. And singing familiar songs makes your job as an entertainer easier. You don't have to worry about *teaching* the audience a song they don't know and, therefore, you can concentrate on communicating the song.

Any song which meets the three basic qualifications above is a potential song for your show. Buy the record and the sheet music for that song and add it to the others you have chosen. When it comes to spending money on your career, there's no better place to start than with records and sheet music. This is one of the first business expenses you should incur. And it's a deductible investment in your career.

(You may be able to save money by exchanging records and sheet music with friends. Also, if you can't find the sheet music for a song, then go directly to the publisher. Often, he will give you both a recording and a lead sheet, i.e., the unpublished sheet music, for no charge.)

When you first begin collecting songs, don't worry about whether you have too many ballads or too many up-tempo songs. Just concentrate on finding good material—material you can identify with, material your audience can identify with and material which is familiar. Later, you can pick and choose from the assortment and gather additional songs if need be.

The next step is to take the record and the sheet music home and begin working on the song.

## APPROACHING A SONG

What is involved in approaching a song?

The first thing to realize is that *attitude* is everything. Depending on what kind of song you are learning, you must decide what attitude(s) you wish to convey while singing the song. Will you be serious, humorous, romantic, thoughtful, vulnerable, sexy? Will you be positive or negative? By positive, we mean offering the listener some hope of affirmative action. Try to find the positive side of every song, especially a sad and painful ballad. If the lyric leaves the audience feeling that all is hopeless and there is no redeeming thought, you should reconsider whether or not to sing the song. Usually, however, you can find a positive thought in even the most depressing song and emphasize that thought with a positive attitude. For example, in the song "Lay Me Down (Roll Me Out To Sea)," the positive action-oriented thought is "I have made a decision to give up. I have come to grips with the fact that our love is a failure and I'm resigned to killing myself. But in so doing, I will end this horrible pain I feel." It's not a pretty thought, but your attitude, if it is positive, can prevent the song from becoming totally depressing.

Before you adopt an attitude for a new song, study the approach of those who have sung the song before you. You may wish to adopt a different attitude, as Barbra Streisand did when she sang "Happy Days Are Here Again" as a melancholy ballad. But before you do anything, understand the feeling most people associate with the song. This is why it's helpful to learn from a record. You can play the record again and again and pick up the nuances in the attitude of the singer.

Practice the song with your musical director or vocal coach. Together, analyze the song and understand its structure.


## INTRODUCTION

There are four fundamental parts to every song. First, there is the introduction, which is the first eight to sixteen bars of the song. This is where the story begins. Your character or attitude is established. Your objective or motivation, whatever it may be, is stated. The scene is set for a dramatic moment to develop.

Don't confuse the lyrical introduction of a song with the *instrumental* introduction. Many records, for example, have an instrumental signature at the beginning which immediately identifies the song. It may be played on a piano, a saxophone, a steel guitar, violins or any number of other instruments. If you wish, try to duplicate the sound of that introduction when you perform the song so the audience will recognize and be drawn into the song right away. Of course, you also should note and try to duplicate other licks, solos or special sound effects which are widely recognized as being part of the song. These licks usually are not written in the sheet music, so you must copy them from the recording.

## DEVELOPMENT

Next, there's the development of the song. The idea and melody of a song is developed in the verses, chorus, bridge and sometimes the instrumental interlude in the song. The first verse, like the first paragraph of a news story, should set the scene and reveal the players. Each subsequent verse must advance the story or the sentiment of the song. The last verse should complete the story or resolve the thought behind the song. The chorus should contain the overriding message or the point of the song, and it should be the most memorable part of the lyric and the strongest part of the melody. The chorus often is referred to as the "hook," a "hook" being a catchy, repetitive musical phrase. Melodically and lyrically the chorus should be the foundation on which the song is built. It should stay with the listener. And, of course, it should differ from the verses. The bridge is a departure—melodically and lyrically—from the verses and the choruses. It may provide relief or emphasis. An *instrumental* bridge, solo or musical interlude further develops the song melodically by adding dimension, color or texture.

## CLIMAX

Now comes the climax of the song. The climax is the moment when your objective is attained, a solution is found or, with greater determination, you re-state the problem. It is important that you understand when you have reached this point in the song. Without this realization, the dramatic effect is dissipated. Of course, the climax is more obvious in a dramatic ballad than it is in a rock song, but every song can and should have a climactic peak.

## ENDING

Finally, once the song has developed and built to a climax, it must have an *ending.* It sounds obvious, but the majority of pop records do *not* have endings—the song fades out. You can't very well do a fade-out on stage, so give each song an ending. Button it up. The ending lets the audience know the song is finished and, more importantly, it tells them when to applaud.

The audience should not be surprised by an ending, whether it's loud or soft. Either through your body movement, what the band does, lyrically, or how you hold the last notes of the song, let the audience know—"Here comes the ending." Then end the song. And then say by what you do (by bowing, holding out your hands or looking directly at the audience), "There is was." (See chart pg. 68, then charts pgs. 64–67.)

## ROUTINING A SONG

Once you have studied the structure of a song—its introduction, development, climax and ending—you then must *routine* or arrange the song for performance. In other words, working with your musical director and/or vocal coach, you must decide how many verses and choruses you are going to sing, determine the most effective order in

## SPECIFIC DIAGRAM OF A SONG
### *Standard Song

| | A SECTION | A SECTION | B SECTION | A SECTION |
|---|---|---|---|---|
| **Music** | 1st 8 bars | 2nd 8 bars | Bridge—3rd 8 bars | Last 8 bars |
| **Musical Idea** | Introduction | More intro, beginning of development | Development to climax | Possible more development to climax and ending or just ending if climax was reached in bridge |
| **Lyrical Idea** | Here's my situation | And another thing | This is what I'm going to do about it | My problem has been resolved |
| **Singers Interpretation** | Sing melody simply. A statement of intent and objectives. Give the attitude and set the scene, draw them in | Tell more of the story, add a few licks and begin intensity growth | Build intensity to the climax, make your decision known, drive the point home | Let the audience know your committed to your decision and are resolved to see it through |
| **Stage Movement** | Simple, few or no gestures—center stage | Move to another area | Change body attitude, show something new | Back to original position |
| **Orchestration Idea** | Simple, one instrument then add another | Full group, possible different lines | Full group—unison lines building to as full as possible | Full group—unison lines building to as full as possible |
| **Orchestration example (quartet)** | Guitar accompaniment 1st 4 bars add bass in bar 5 | Add piano and drums, guitar plays counter-melody | All play full chords and lines in octaves | All play full chords and lines in octaves |

*To better understand this graph, think if through using the lyrics of a standard ABA song such as "I'm in the Mood for Love" or "Sentimental Journey."

65

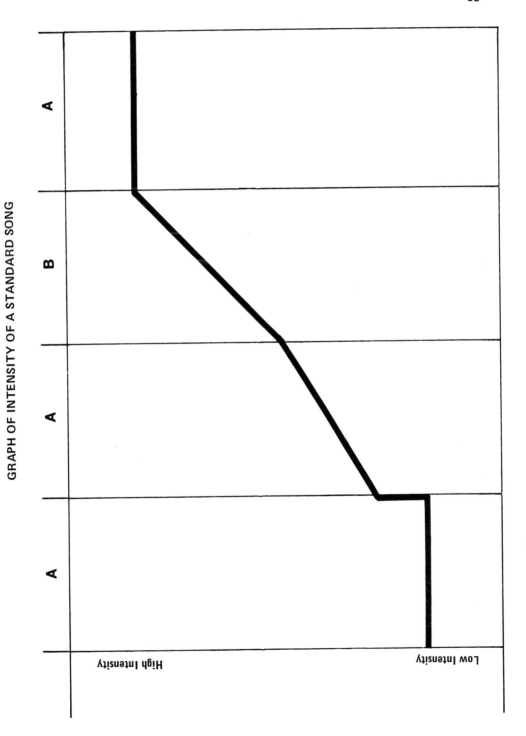

GRAPH OF INTENSITY OF A STANDARD SONG

## SPECIFIC DIAGRAM OF A SONG
### *Contemporary Song

| | A SECTION | B SECTION | A SECTION | B SECTION | B SECTION |
|---|---|---|---|---|---|
| Music | 8 bars—verse | 8 bars—chorus | 8 bars—verse | 8 bars—chorus | 8 bars—chorus |
| Musical Idea | Introduction | Main Theme | Development | Climax | Ending |
| Lyrical Idea | Here's my situation | Here's my solution | And another thing | My conclusion still is | My conclusion is even more sure |
| Singers Interpretation | Sing the song the way it is commonly heard | This is the hook, sing it straight, never vary the notes | More story, greater intensity you can add a few licks | Restate conclusion—hook should be a little stronger than 1st time | Restate hook as the strongest statement with conviction |
| Stage Movement | Stage left | Center stage | Stage right | Center stage, a little up stage | Center stage, move down stage |
| Orchestration Idea | Set the mood | Full sound but leave room to build | As 1st A but add new color in sound | Full sound | Fullest sound |
| Orchestration example (quartet) | Full group—all harmonic background—subtle | Full group—total support of melody | Full group—guitar playing counter-melody | Full group—bass line embellished | Full group—volume up, drum fills |

*To better understand this graph, think it through using the lyrics of a contemporary song such as "Feelings."

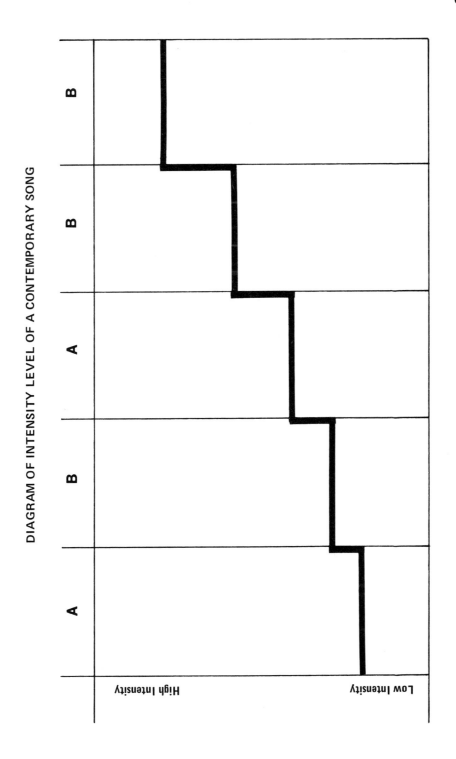

DIAGRAM OF INTENSITY LEVEL OF A CONTEMPORARY SONG

BASIC DIAGRAM OF A SONG AND GRAPH OF INTENSITY

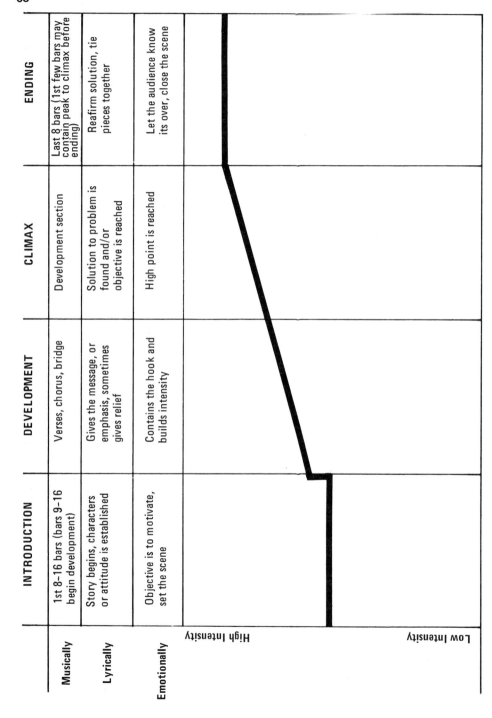

|  | INTRODUCTION | DEVELOPMENT | CLIMAX | ENDING |
|---|---|---|---|---|
| **Musically** | 1st 8–16 bars (bars 9–16 begin development) | Verses, chorus, bridge | Development section | Last 8 bars (1st few bars may contain peak to climax before ending) |
| **Lyrically** | Story begins, characters or attitude is established | Gives the message, or emphasis, sometimes gives relief | Solution to problem is found and/or objective is reached | Reafirm solution, tie pieces together |
| **Emotionally** | Objective is to motivate, set the scene | Contains the hook and builds intensity | High point is reached | Let the audience know its over, close the scene |

High Intensity

Low Intensity

which to sing them and the bridge, if any, and decide where to place instrumental solos and modulations (key changes), if any. For example, you may wish to combine verses to shorten a song, thereby making it more effective in "live" performance; or you may wish to drop a chorus or two. Eliminating long instrumental solos generally is a good idea when you're singing in front of an audience because, by and large, the singer has got egg on his face when the orchestra (or band) is being beautiful. Unless you're going to feature the orchestra or unless you've got something to say or do (like go off-stage) while they're playing, you probably will want to cut out any unnecessary orchestral or instrumental breaks or "turnarounds" when you're routining a song for the stage. Also, you may wish to add a modulation (key change) on the final chorus to give the song "lift" and greater impact. And, of course, in the process of routining each song, you have an opportunity to discover the best way to phrase the lyric and add your own interpretation.

When routining songs, avoid these common pitfalls: (1) Don't use unnecessary vocal affectations such as backphrasing. Backphrasing, where you start the lyric line *later* than it's written and then catch up to the beat, was popular among jazz singers in the 40s and also was fashionable at one time among saloon singers and crooners. The pause when you backphrase actually creates an artificial emphasis, and today this is considered corny in pop singing. Generally, it is best to sing right on the beat or in front of the beat; (2) Be aware that when you drastically alter the tempo or structure of a song it may lose its impact and feeling; and (3) Don't change the melody of a song the first time through or it won't be recognizable. (See charts pgs. 70–73.)


## MUSICAL TREATMENTS

Here are some suggestions for musical treatments:

1. Start the song with the chorus (the "hook") or the bridge to give the song more energy or to get immediate audience response.

BASIC ROUTINE OF A STANDARD SONG AND GRAPH OF INTENSITY

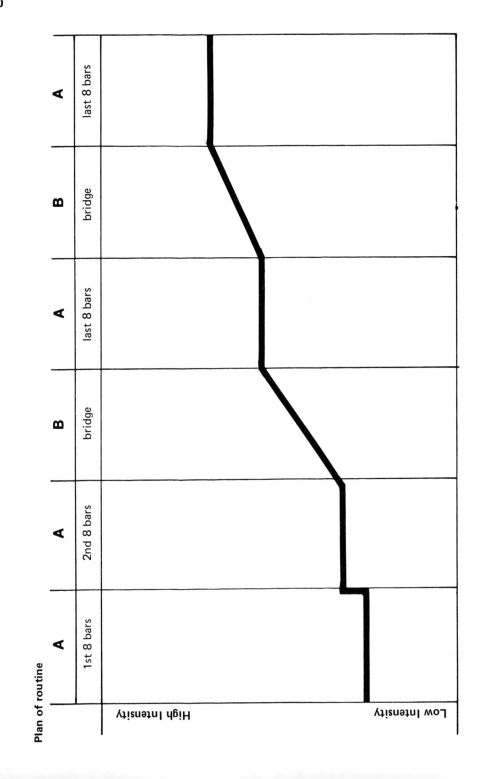

BASIC ROUTINE OF A CONTEMPORARY SONG AND GRAPH OF INTENSITY

Plan of routine

| B | A | B | A | B | B |
|---|---|---|---|---|---|
| Start with hook | 1st verse | hook | 2nd verse | hook | hook |

High Intensity

Low Intensity

## MORE SPECIFIC ROUTINE OF A STANDARD SONG AND GRAPH OF INTENSITY

**Plan of routine**

| A | A | B | A | Transition | Bridge | A |
|---|---|---|---|---|---|---|
| Speak lyric 1st 8 bars w/guitar ad-lib | Sing—add tempo add bass and piano | Add drums build intensity | Full sound same feeling | 2 bar modulation 1 step higher | change 4/4 feel to 12/8 and start to drive | Keep intensity up to big ending |

Intensity graph: High Intensity / Low Intensity

MORE SPECIFIC ROUTINE OF A CONTEMPORARY SONG AND GRAPH OF INTENSITY

Plan of routine

| Intro. | A | B | Transition | B | Transition | B |
|---|---|---|---|---|---|---|
| Instrumental intro. 4 bars including part of the hook | Verse with light accompaniment | Chorus with heavy accompaniment | Instrumental 2 bars—condensed version of hook modulation up 1/2 step | Chorus building with instrumental fills | Abrupt modulation up 1/2 step in last 3 beats of chorus with heavy drum fills | Chorus very heavy with instrumental fills constantly building |

High Intensity — Low Intensity

2. Try speaking thc lyric if it is a great lyric. Harry Chapin's song, "Cat's In The Cradle" is a good vehicle for this type of treatment.
3. Change the *feel* (rhythm) of the song. Then speed it up or slow it down to see how the *tempo* affects the interpretation.
4. Try starting a song *ad lib* or, in other words, out of tempo with just piano or guitar. This draws the listener into the song.
5. Use modulations (key changes) to give the song lift and make it bigger.
6. In a ballad, try changing the rhythm from a soft or lilting 4/4 time to a harder, stronger feel to drive it home. Or try starting in 4/4 and building into 12/8 for emphasis.


**INTERPRETATION**

How you interpret a song is extremely important in pop singing. You must make every song your own. You must tailor the song to fit you, and you must sing it as though it is a part of you.

Look at a song as a collection of images or pictures. Let each phrase paint a little picture. And each time you sing that phrase, see the picture in your mind. Visualize the song, for every good song is, as Mac Davis put it, a "word movie."

Try paraphrasing the lyric. In other words, while you are singing the song, fill in additional dialogue that might be going on between the people in the song. Do this in your mind. Tell yourself the story of the song while you sing it. Add the detail and feeling you think lies behind the lyric.

Sense memory also can help you interpret a song. If it is a sad song, recall a sad time in your life. Use that recalled emotion in the song. John Stewart, one of California's finest singer-songwriters, uses sense memory when he sings his classic song, "Mother Country." The song is about an old man who is going blind, but who insists on driving his favorite harness racing horse, The Old Campaigner, one more time. Before John sings the line, "Here she comes/The Old Campaigner/With

E. A. Stuart right behind," he waits until he actually can see the race track and the horse in his mind. John grew up around race tracks and he uses his sense memory—the sight, sounds and smell of the remembered experience there—to make the song come alive. It's so effective, John takes his audience right with him and they, too, can see the old man's final moment of glory.

## PURPOSE

Every song you sing must have a purpose. There must be a reason for singing it. The song either should convey happiness, sadness or melancholy, humor or satire, a provocative thought, an expression of love or some personal insight into life. If it's a happy song, it really has to be happy, it can't be wishy-washy. You've got to be happy singing it. Barry Manilow's "It's A Miracle" is a good example of an explosion of happiness. If you're going to do a song to make people think, give them something to think about. If you're going to do an uplifting song, build it to a point which is truly uplifting. Don't pull your punches. Define in your mind the purpose of each and every song, then commit yourself to that purpose with everything you've got when you sing the song.

The purpose of each song should become clear to the audience. When you're singing, keep in mind that the audience is picking up on two things all the time—your *intent* and your *intensity*. Intent is the reason, the purpose, for singing the song, what you hope to accomplish and what effect you hope it will have on the listener. Intensity, which we will discuss in more detail later, is the size, the power or the energy which you put behind the actual performance. Don't confuse intent and intensity. You know from speaking (and the same rule applies to singing) that you can say something very softly but say it with such clear intent that the effect is greater than if you shouted it. On stage, your intent must be absolutely clear at all times in everything you sing, say or do.

## CREATING A MOOD

When approaching a song, you also must think about creating a mood with that song. Choose a mood which suits the song or, better yet, which is suggested by the song itself. Then deliberately go about setting that mood.

What tools can you use to create a mood?

Attitude is the first tool. More than anything, the attitude you adopt for the song will become the vehicle through which the mood is set. If you are playing a dramatic part in a play, then your attitude is dictated by the role you're playing. The role gives you the motivation, the words you say, the intent, even how to move and gesture. But as a pop singer, you have no predetermined role. You're naked. You have to supply the attitude, the motivation, the words you say, the intent and so on. And your show must become a series of attitudes, well-defined and well-developed.

Tempo and rhythm also are tools. By rhythm, we mean the *feel*—disco, country, rock, swing, waltz, etc. The rhythm of the song helps dictate your attitude. If it's swing, it suggests you be loose, carefree and easy. If the rhythm is disco or rock, it suggests you be more energetic, more purposeful, perhaps even more "macho." Some rhythms make you want to strut, others make you want to stroll or sway. So, the rhythmic feel you choose for a song has a lot to do with the mood the song creates.

Tempo is the speed or pace of the song, literally the timing. If you slow down the tempo, it makes the lyric more important. If you speed up the tempo, it makes the lyric less important. If a song has weight and you do it too fast, it will seem flippant and the seriousness will be lost. When you feel that a song isn't riding in a groove (the best tempo), slow it down. The slower tempo will make you commit yourself more to the lyric. Experiment with tempos; don't get locked into a particular tempo just because someone tells you it's right. During a performance, if the band or orchestra plays a song too slow, you may find it disconcerting. Suddenly, you become aware of great, gaping holes between phrases. If you fill in those holes with attitude and concentrate on a greater commitment to the lyric, you'll be able to relax and enjoy the slower tempo more readily. The object, of course, is to set the correct tempo for each song and do the song at that tempo each time.

The mood of a song also is affected by the *key* in which you sing it. If you want to speak a lyric or phrase it like you're speaking, set the key down in your speaking range. The simplest way to do this is to go to the piano and talk the lyric through. Find the key for your speaking voice, but be sure it's not too high. Otherwise your speaking will become "singy."

Conversely, if you set the key for a song too low, you will have difficulty producing the kind of sustained tones you want when singing. If you are practicing by yourself and are not able to simulate a performing situation, be aware that you usually can sing a half-step higher on stage under performing conditions. For some reason, probably adrenalin, you'll be able to handle a slightly higher key on stage than you will in your living room.

Never set a key so high that you can't sing comfortably. Many singers prefer higher keys because they think their voices sound more commercial and more exciting up high. To some extent, this is true. But you must strike a reasonable balance. Singing above your natural range causes vocal fatigue and, in some cases, damage. In the end, what you may gain by having a higher voice is not worth it. Singing in a lower key involves less vocal energy and usually is associated with a more intimate, sensual feeling. Low notes are sexy.

## EMOTIONAL INVESTMENT

Remember this: there are many pop singers who don't have great voices, yet are very successful. Why? Because they *sell* the song. They have an attitude. They create a mood. They act out the story. They personalize the story. When they sing, it is as though they are telling you something that happened to them. They make the song fit the way a tailor makes a suit fit.

If you write and sing your own songs, automatically you have a greater involvement, a greater investment in what you're singing. The songwriter's own songs are like windows into his or her life. When you sing your own songs, not only are you necessarily more vulnerable (you put your work up for judgment), but also you probably are revealing more of yourself.

When you sing other people's songs, you must make it appear (and it should be so) that you are as involved in the song as the person who wrote it. It has to mean as much to you as it did to the writer. This is why you must make every song your own. Make an emotional investment in it. Put your stamp on it.

When approaching a *love song,* always try to sing the essence of what is being said in the lyric. Sing *sensuality* into the lyric. The lyric in many contemporary love songs already is suggestive. Don't let that scare you. Capitalize on it. Make what is suggestive come to life in your mind—become the person in the song.

Sometimes in love songs, understating your vocal intensity is appealing. But never understate your intent. Keep in mind when you're singing a love song that your intent is loving, being loved or making love.

Singers of love songs dating back to Al Jolson have recognized the importance of this. When Jolson sang "I'd walk a million miles for one of your smiles" in the song "Mammy," he sang it as though he were saying, "I'd do anything to be with you, to be in your warm embrace." That's the feeling he conveyed. When Donna Summer sings "Love to Love You, Baby," she means it. The lyric, though not explicitly sexual, takes on sexual connotations because of the way she delivers it. She's not afraid to reveal that part of herself. If you are singing the Dan Hill song, "Sometimes When We Touch," remember that, in reality, you are singing "Sometimes when we *make love.*" Don't play it safe. Dare to be sensual and provocative.

In summary, it is not absolutely necessary to have a great voice to be a pop singing star. An ordinary voice, on key and without major faults, is good enough vocal equipment with which to sing most pop songs. Beyond that, it is what you bring to the songs—your attitude, mood, emotional investment, commitment, believability—that counts.

CHAPTER 4

# PREPARING YOUR ACT

*"The journey of a thousand miles
begins with the first step."*

—*Anonymous (Chinese)*

**It may be possible** to manufacture a singing entertainer in much the same way as you would any other product. A producer (literally one who turns raw materials into useful articles) with enough experience and expertise in all the various aspects of the musical entertainment business conceivably could take any reasonably attractive and talented singer and make him or her a "star." The producer could arrange for everything—speech, voice, acting and dancing lessons, a musical director, arranger and musicians. The producer could choose all the songs for the singer (and have songs written), write and stage the act (or have it written and staged) and then promote and sell the finished product. In short, the right producer could take a singer who is a diamond in the rough and turn him into a finely polished gem—all the singer would have to do is be competent enough to do what is expected of him at all times.

Yet, while in theory it may be possible to manufacture a singing entertainer, in practice it is not a very realistic proposition. Nor is it done very often. First of all, producers capable of actually propelling someone from rags to riches are hard to find. And more importantly, if you could find one, there is no guarantee your starmaker would be able to make you the kind of star you want to be. Finally, the hidden cost to the performer of allowing someone to completely take over his or her career would be incalculable. The singer would not enjoy the sense of accomplishment which comes with struggling and succeeding and, in the end, might find manufactured stardom to be an empty, hollow existence.

Moreover, it is not desirable in the long run to be someone else's creation, a product without any intrinsic identity of its own. Numerous people will play key roles in your evolution as a singing entertainer—their services, at times, will be indespensible—but *you* must be your own producer. Especially in the beginning, you must be the one who figures out how to develop whatever raw talent you have into a polished, finished product. Not only is this the most realistic way to proceed, but also it is by far the most rewarding and enriching.

## FINDING OUT WHO YOU ARE

The essence of your career is you. Whether you gain prominence through television, motion pictures or recording, the core of your career remains who you are, what you do and how people react to you. And there is no better way to discover and develop yourself than through personal appearances.

By performing in front of audiences, you find out what personality, attitudes, material and delivery works for you. You discover not only how to perform, but also how to *be.* You find yourself. You define what kind of product you are. And in so doing, you discover that which ultimately will make you desirable, saleable and successful in other media—television, recording and film.

The key to a successful career as a singing entertainer is combining the ability to captivate and entertain an audience in a live performance situation with enough mass media exposure to create and insure a demand for such performances. Eventually, one kind of performing begins to feed and support the other until finally you are capable of working in, and there is demand for you in, all areas of show business.

What is involved in preparing for a live performance?

Whether you are going to sing in Joe's Bar & Grill, a coffee house or the main room of the Las Vegas Hilton, you must put together an act. In other words, you must have a *purpose* for performing, a *plan* for your performance and a *goal* you want to achieve. You must know before you go on stage what you're going to sing, what you're going to say, how you're going to act, what you're going to wear, how you're going to move, how you're going to get the audience to listen to and respond.

Your purpose, as we have discussed earlier, is to entertain people, touch them in some way, make them laugh or perhaps cry but, above all, make them feel good about their lives. But you can accomplish this overwhelming task only if the audience identifies with your music and with you as a person. And for a performance to be a complete success, you must emerge as a person out in front of your material. The end product of your performance—your music, vocal ability, wardrobe, sets, lighting, sound—should be a picture of you the way you want the audience to see you.

But what should that picture look like? Who are you going to be on stage? What do you want to project?

These are fundamental questions every singer should consider when preparing to perform. If you're normal, you are not one thing. You are many things. Your personality is comprised of many different feelings and attitudes. At different times, you may be energetic, fun-loving, humorous, irritable, jealous, rude, joyful, naive, generous, guilt-ridden, impatient or filthy-minded. You must decide which of these many aspects of your personality you want to use when you're entertaining and which facets of your personality will help you achieve your purpose.

Make a list of the different sides to your personality which you wish to use on stage. List the things you would like the audience to see in you. Such a list might look like this:

1. I want the audience to see the side of me that is happy;
2. I want them to see that I have the ability (depth) to *feel* things;
3. I want them to see that I don't take myself too seriously and that I have a sense of humor about myself;
4. I want them to see the side of me that loves them;
5. I want them to see the side of me that enjoys what I'm doing;
6. I want them to see that I'm clever, quick-thinking and on top of things;
7. I want them to see the sexual and sensual sides of me;
8. I want them to see the romantic and sensitive sides of me;
9. I want them to see that they can trust me and trust our friend-ship; and
10. I want them to see that I have talent.

Now, make a list of the sides to your personality that you don't want to use on stage. List what you don't want the audience to see. Your list might look like this:

1. I don't want the audience to see my petty nature, the perfectionist side of me which they might not understand or the fact that I'm basically a worrier;
2. I don't want them to see my insecurities unless, by revealing them, the audience will identify with me and like me better;
3. I don't want them to know my sexual fantasies;
4. I don't want them to see me out of control on stage or not in command of the situation; and
5. I don't want them to see the jealous side of me, or the hateful, bitter, caustic or negative side of me, unless it can be used for comedy.

Once you have clarified in your own mind which qualities you want to project on stage and which you want to conceal, then you will begin to come into focus as an individual. You will have drawn the basic outline for the picture of yourself you wish to paint for your audience.

## INDIVIDUALITY

You now can proceed with formulating a *plan* for your performance. You can choose the songs you're going to sing and begin putting them together in a way that will make an entertaining show.

Assuming you already have read Chapter Three, you know what criteria you should use in choosing material for your act. You must choose (a) songs for which you have strong feelings; (b) songs which will move your audience; and (c) in general, songs which are familiar. But let's go a step further. Each song you choose also must be a vehicle for your particular talents. By this we mean each song first must be stageworthy and then must add to the picture of yourself which you are trying to paint for your audience.

For example, if you have a list of 20 familiar songs, each of which is a contender for your show, you may find some are not "live performance songs." In other words, there will be some which are not theatrical enough, not adaptable to the stage. Occasionally this is true of songs which have been major hit records. For one reason or another, when you try to sing this kind of song "live," it doesn't work. And if you try to force such a song to be stageworthy, usually you end up destroying the qualities which made the song effective in the first place. Songs of this type never will be effective vehicles for your talents.

Once you know a song is stageworthy, however, then you must be sure it contributes in some way to the development of your overall image or personality (some call it "style"). Even though eighty to ninety percent of the songs in your act should be well-known contemporary songs, each one also must be uniquely suited to your personality, attitude and ability. The net effect should be to make a cohesive statement about you and enable you to emerge as an individual. Build individuality into your act at every opportunity for, without it, you will end up being indistinguishable from every other singer around. Don't be content with being a "juke box that tells jokes." Give your act a point of view.

## BUYING MATERIAL

Many singing entertainers buy material—jokes, ideas for medleys or audience participation segments, special musical material, concepts for staging and choreographing production numbers. There are hundreds of professional writers, arrangers and choreographers who create material for working entertainers. But in the beginning, large sums of money spent on buying material for your act usually is not a very good investment. You first must experiment with attitudes and production ideas of your own which will help define who you are as a performer. Only then will you have some basis for deciding whether a suggested piece of material is right for you.

At some point in your career, however, it may not be unwise to buy material. If you're opening for the first time in a main room in Las Vegas, for example, and you don't have a strong audience participation segment in your show or your show is lacking in production values customarily seen in Las Vegas, then you would be foolish not to have material written. There are a number of classic stories about big-name personalities who have tried to play Las Vegas without first putting together an act. The result is always the same—no matter how famous the personality or how well received in other areas of show business, without an act, he or she bombs.

If and when you do decide to purchase material, be aware that the cost of having things written can be astronomical. It is not unusual for an established choreographer to ask $3,500 to conceive and choreograph *one* number. Well-known comedy writers ask as much as $2,500 for three pages of jokes. The *concept* for a medley may cost $500. Then, you've got to have an arranger orchestrate it and have a copyist write it out for all of the individual members of your band or orchestra. That's another $1,000, at least. If you have your entire act written, from beginning to end, conservatively it could cost as much as $50,000.

Thus, in the early going, you will be far better off spending time, rather than money, creating material for yourself. Take the ideas you have and develop them as best you can. An idea does not have to be expensive or complicated to work. And when you're playing a Holiday

Inn lounge or the bar in some steak house, an overly-ambitious and elaborately produced act isn't necessary. It would be too big for the room. So, stick to the basics. Concentrate on picking the best songs for you. Develop simple ideas for audience participation. Come up with your own ideas for medleys.

## MEDLEYS

A medley is a musical arrangement in which several songs having something in common are strung together to form one musical composition. A medley can be comprised of hit songs by a particular artist. A medley can be made out of love songs, work songs or songs about cities and states. Medleys also can be based on musical styles, for instance, a medley of country songs, disco songs or songs from the 1950s.

What is the purpose of a medley?

Before you go wild and fill up your show with one medley after another, understand the two basic functions of the medley. First, the medley helps move the show along. Hence, it is a device to be used in *pacing* the show. Second, the medley is designed to *increase audience response.* Weaving several different songs together demonstrates your versatility as a singer. The medley also appears to give the audience more music for its money. A strong medley will appear to be a tour de force by the singer and the audience will react to it much more favorably than they would to any one of the songs separately. But be careful not to over-use medleys. Ask yourself if the medley really is needed for pacing or to boost audience reaction at a certain point in the show.

Here are five rules to follow when creating a medley:

1. The premise of the medley must be clear, and it must be followed all the way through. If the premise is a nostalgic look at the 1950s, obviously you shouldn't throw in a song from the 1940s or the 1960s. Use the nostalgic "blockbusters" from the period. State the

premise clearly with the first song, and then be sure each subsequent song reinforces and develops the premise.

2. Limit the medley to a maximum of 6 or 7 minutes. Medleys which go on for more than seven minutes, no matter how impressively written or performed, are too long. And if a medley is too long, the audience either will forget the premise or won't care anymore by the time you get to the end.

3. Where possible, include only the most familiar sections of each song being used in the medley. By its nature, the medley form doesn't allow you to sing any of the songs in their entirety, so you must be sure that the parts you are singing are instantly recognizable.

4. A good medley should have a consistent, smooth musical flow while, at the same time, utilizing a variety of tempos and rhythms. But the songs should relate to each other musically as well as lyrically, so it shouldn't try to encompass too many styles or changes in tempo or it will seem disjointed.

5. Finally, a medley must have a lyric or musical treatment at the end which, in some way, re-states the premise and wraps up the entire piece. As in a single song, a medley should build to a climax and finish with an effective ending.

To start you thinking about concepts for medleys, here are a few suggestions:

*A medley of songs from recent major motion pictures.* The premise is that good music, once again, is coming from the movies. The songs should be taken from the most popular movies of the previous year or two, and each song should be well-known enough to get applause when you start it. The medley should finish with the most popular song of the whole group. Use no more than 5 songs. Tempos should be varied, but the medley should flow lyrically from song to song.

*A medley-tribute to a major artist or composer.* Use only the artist or composer's major hits. Tempos should vary. Again, each song lyrically should relate to the next. For example, if the medley were a tribute to Barry Manilow, the lyric theme throughout would be love—falling in love, losing love, finding love and so on. Perhaps you could put a dramatic reading in the middle which says something the artist or composer really believes or has said. This medley should be built around an artist or composer the audience has feeling for, and it should not be more than 6 minutes long. End it big.

*A nostalgia medley.* The premise could be nostalgia about a certain part of the country. For example, a medley of songs about where you grew up. Again, it might be appropriate to include a short dramatic reading about the area. Or the premise could be nostalgia for the songs and musical styles of another era such as the '40s, the '50s or the '60s. Make sure all the songs are well-known so that the piece will bring back memories for everyone. Nostalgia only works if it touches the majority of your audience. Songs of the South might grab people from the South, but the rest of the audience will feel left out, unless you can wrap up the medley with some universal theme about America. Whatever form of nostalgia you choose to deal with, be sure you have a song at the end which re-states the premise and concludes the segment.

Work over concepts for medleys with your musical director. He or she will be the best judge of whether an idea can be made to work musically; and together you can determine whether it will work vocally for you. When you're looking for or developing material, it's always useful to study other performers. Not that you would want to do what they're doing but watching other singing entertainers will give you a better idea of what the possibilities are. You also might get ideas for medleys or audience participation segments by watching television variety shows, game shows and entertainment-talk shows.


## AUDIENCE PARTICIPATION

Speaking at JDSSC in 1978, John Davidson explained his approach to audience participation:

"When I first started doing live performances as a singing entertainer, I wanted to just get up on stage and sing song after song. But Bob Banner, the TV producer I was working with at the time, always insisted that I develop 'talk spots.' In fact, it was Banner's ideas to do the audience participation segment in my show in which I sing the songs that were popular when people first fell in love. Over the years, reviewers have said that this segment is conceptually as worthy and timeless a piece of material as any singer could hope to have, and I guess they're right. It has become a sort of trademark.

"The segment is called 'They're Playing Our Song' and here is how it works: We picked the three most popular songs from each of the years from 1920 to 1975 (a total of 165 songs) and put them into a three-song medley for each year. All of the music is in a book for the orchestra. At a certain point in my show, I go into the audience and ask couples what year they fell in love. I get a year, say 1947, and that is the cue for my musical director to pull out the three-song medley for 1947. While I tell a few jokes and find out where the couple is from, my conductor plays enough of the melody from the first song to refresh my memory. Then I sing the medley. During a typical performance, I'll sing the medleys from two or three years, before returning to the stage. It is interesting to note that this type of participation segment not only involves the audience but also makes effective use of the medley form.

"Another audience participation segment which I have found to be successful is what I call 'The Opera Bit.' The concept was inspired by comedian Don Rickles. Here's how it works: I pick a man in the audience, usually one who is slightly over-weight because I've found heavier people generally have a better sense of humor about themselves. I bring him to the stage, and I explain that we are going to act out an opera together. I sing the set-up and everything I say during the bit in a phony sort of opera voice, and I ask him to respond the same way. Most people pick right up on the idea and try to sing in an operatic voice. I set the scene. I tell the man that he has just come home from work to find me in his bedroom with his wife—we've been making love for three solid hours. Then I ask the man what he thinks of that. Usually, no matter what he says ('You're a better man than I am . . .'), it's funny. One problem with this kind of segment is that, once you have someone on stage, you must have a pay-off (a finish) to end the segment and send them back into the audience. You have to pick the high point. In the case of 'The Opera Bit,' I take the biggest laugh and simply end it there. The orchestra plays a musical tag while I ask the audience to applaud him."

These two examples of audience participation segments should give you an idea of how to put together a segment of your own. Perhaps you can find a variation on these themes and make them work for you.

## LENGTH OF ACT

In case it isn't already obvious, at the outset, you must involve your musical director in the process of assembling all the various types of material you will be using in your act. He or she can help you decide which songs will be the most effective vehicles for you, and he or she will be able to help you conceive and arrange whatever medleys or audience participation segments you may wish to include in your show. If you don't have a musical director, put together the elements yourself and, where necessary, work with a musician or an arranger who can write out the music ("charts") you need. It is possible to design an effective act using extremely simple ideas. So, don't get carried away. A successful act depends not so much on the complexity of its ingredients but rather on the execution of those ingredients. In the final analysis, it is your *choices* which are important—the right song, medley or audience participation number in the right place at the right time. A simply conceived act performed with proper *pacing,* a subject with which we deal in chapter six, can be as impressive, if not more so, than an overly-ambitious one.

In the beginning, assemble a thirty-minute act. And make those 30 minutes "dynamite." In most situations, this will be enough. Then, gradually expand your act so that you're able to do approximately 60 to 75 minutes. But, as you do this, don't sacrifice quality for quantity. Remember that every song or musical segment in the show must have a purpose in terms of the overall pacing of your show.

As an opening act in nightclubs, supper clubs or concerts, you only will be expected to do about 25 to 30 minutes before the headliner, or main act, comes on. Usually, a headliner will do an hour or an hour and 15 minutes. In smaller venues, such as cocktail lounges or restaurants where you are the only attraction, you may be expected to do as many as four, 45-minute performances per night. And in these types of engagements, typically there is little or no "turnover" in the audience. That is, the same people may remain in your audience all night long. If this is the case, add enough songs or musical segments to your basic 30-minute act to make it run 45 minutes. Then, create a *second* act or "set" of the same length. This second "set" can be a variation on the first. Keep the same structure and pacing, but change the songs. When you change a song, though, be sure you replace it with a similar song which fits in that spot.

In other words, put in songs which will have the same effect and accomplish the same purpose as the original songs. In restaurants and lounges, you need at least two different "sets" in order to avoid sounding repetitious.


## SOUND

We live in a technological age when audiences expect high quality sound reproduction in live situations. As a singing entertainer, you must recognize the importance of having a good public address system, whether you are performing in concert, in nightclubs and supper clubs, or in small lounges or restaurants. Because sound is so important in live performances, most clubs, lounges and concert halls already are equipped with adequate or, in some cases, elaborate sound systems. Still, the only way to be certain that you will have consistently high quality sound wherever you go is to carry your own, self-contained system.

When you're starting out, it may not be necessary or financially feasible to buy your own sound system. But as you progress and your requirements for sound amplification become more important to you, purchasing a portable PA system is one of the best investments you can make in your career. The most popular brand names in sound equipment for pop singers and musicians are Shure, JBL Laboratories, Altec-Lansing, Peavey, Ampeg and Fender. Depending on the manufacturer, the size of the system and the degree of electronic sophistication, a sound system can cost anywhere from $2,000 to $250,000. Large showrooms, such as those found in Las Vegas, often have as much as $500,000 invested in sound equipment alone. Some rock bands and popular recording artists carry enough sound equipment to fill two or three 18-wheeler semis, each the size of a large moving van.

But what kind of sound system do you need?

Basically, you need a sound system which has the following components: (1) Two or four audience speaker columns; (2) A power amplifier capable of pushing sound through ("driving") the speakers; (3) A six or eight channel microphone mixer ("brain") which has separate volume and tone (treble, midrange and bass) controls, plus reverb or echo, for each channel; (4) Six or eight microphones and stands; and (5) One or two on stage monitor speakers.

Obviously, if you're working in front of a 26-piece orchestra or even a 10-piece band with background singers, the above system would be inadequate in terms of the number of microphones needed. If you're playing the Forum in Inglewood, California (on the order of 15,000 seats), such a system would be woefully inadequate in terms of its power, i.e., its ability to fill the room with sound. But assuming you are singing in front of a four to six piece group, and you are playing to anywhere from 100 to 1,000 seats, a quality system with the components listed above usually will suffice.

The function of the microphones, speakers, amplifiers, stage monitors, and mixing board should be obvious. But several points can be made here. Always locate the audience speakers *near the stage* on both sides. The sound should come from the stage, not from the back of the room, the sides or from the ceiling. The audience has to look at the stage to see you, and they should have to face the stage to *hear* you. Voice monitors on stage, so that you can hear yourself sing, are essential. Even though the audience may be hearing you perfectly, when the band or orchestra is playing and you are behind the audience speakers, it's virtually impossible to hear your own voice without monitor speakers. Stage monitors are one of the most important tools of our trade. Just try singing without them some time and you'll see what we mean.

Echo or reverb also is an integral part of the contemporary pop singer's sound. The right amount of echo on your vocal makes your voice sound fuller, smoother and more pleasing to the ear. People are accustomed to this sound. The "dry" voice without echo is not as appealing. Be sure, however, never to use so much echo or reverb that it becomes obvious and distracting. Also, use a little echo in your on-stage monitors and you may like the sound of your voice better.

The location of the microphone mixer ("brain") in the room also is of paramount importance. The mixer and whomever is operating it should be in the center of the room, not back stage or on stage. The reason for this is simple: the best place to get an idea of what the audience is hearing is *in* the room. So, where possible, locate your sound person and mixer board approximately half-way between the front of the stage and the rear of the room roughly on a line with the center of the stage. This is the best location from which to balance the sound from the stage for the majority of the audience.

Several more points about sound. Have you ever noticed that in nightclubs and at concerts there usually is recorded music or background music (Muzak) playing before the show, at intermission and afterwards? This music serves a purpose—it sustains the energy level of the audience. Even though it may be barely audible in the background, the presence of the music is felt. People have to talk a little louder and, hence, they are more animated and energized without even realizing it. At rock concerts, the recorded music played before the show and at intermission often is played at ear-splitting levels. This, too, keeps the crowd's energy level high. So, when you're working in hotel showrooms, lounges or nightclubs where they have Muzak or some other form of recorded background music, turn it up *before* your show. You'll notice the noise level in the room will increase and the audience will become more lively. Of course, before you start your show, you

# SOUND ILLUSTRATION

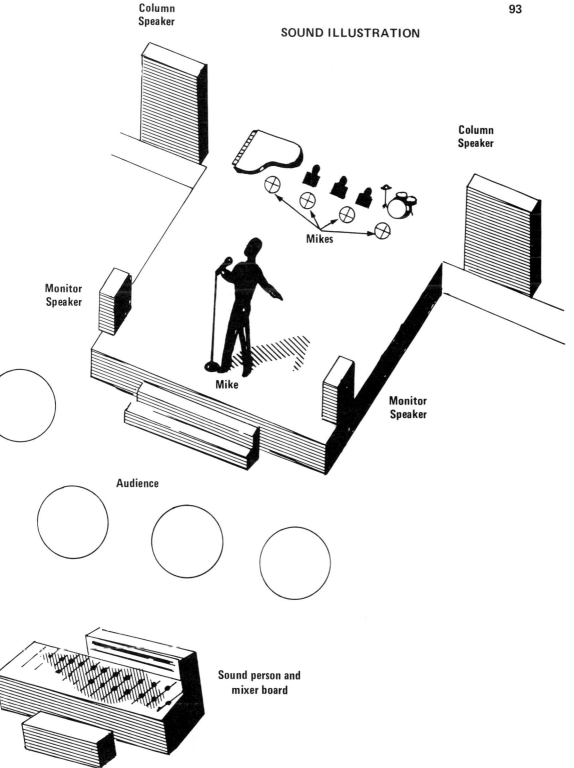

Column
Speaker

Column
Speaker

Mikes

Monitor
Speaker

Mike

Monitor
Speaker

Audience

Sound person and
mixer board

must turn off the Muzak or background music and allow the room to settle down momentarily before you start.

The temperature of a room can have a significant effect on the sound of your show. If the room is too hot, the sound will seem to be muffled, muddy. If the room is too cold, the sound will seem too brash; notes will crackle through the air and sound harder than they should. Though not related to sound, it also is interesting to note that the temperature of the room can affect the way the audience responds. The temperature of the room, after the audience is in and body heat has been taken into account, should be approximately 68 to 70 degrees. If you're going to be working in a room which is too hot or too cold, go to the manager or his representative and insist that the heating or air-conditioning be adjusted accordingly. The best temperature in a room is one which the majority of people in the audience won't notice one way or the other.

One final and very important point about sound equipment. There are dozens of companies who make and sell sound equipment, and prices vary a great deal. But when it comes to buying sound equipment, a good rule is to buy the best components you can. If you can't afford to buy all the components at once, get what you can afford. Buy good speakers. Save your money, then buy a good mixer, and so on. In the end, you may spend more and it may take you longer to acquire a system, but you will have a worthier system which will serve you better for a longer period of time.

## LIGHTING

The purpose of lighting is to tell the audience where to look. Lighting directs the audience's attention. If you are performing in a main room in Las Vegas, Reno, Tahoe or Atlantic City, or you are doing a tour of one-nighters in concert halls around the country, you must hire a lighting designer. But what can you do if you're playing the lounge of a Holiday Inn or a cocktail bar in a restaurant?

Any room, no matter how small or ill-equipped, can be made into a reasonably good showroom with three basic types of lighting. With a "follow spot" light, light "trees" on either side of the stage and a few fixed "specials" in front of the stage, you can transform an otherwise drab stage and make it a serviceable area in which to perform.

A "follow spot"—the best means of directing the audience's attention—is the first type of lighting needed to make an ordinary room into a *show*room. There are two basic types of "follow spots." One type is powered by an incandescent bulb (a high-powered light bulb), and the other is powered by a carbon arc (an electric spark jumping between two terminals). An incandescent type spot, known as a Trouperette, is sufficient in most small rooms. However, the more powerful carbon arc variety, known as a Trouper or Super Trouper, is necessary in larger rooms, auditoriums and arenas. Locate your "follow spot" (Trouperette) at the rear of the room in the center or off to one side so that it has a clear shot at all areas of the stage. Of course, you'll need someone to operate the light when you're on stage, but finding a volunteer to do this shouldn't be too difficult in most cases. It's a good idea if the Trouperette has flesh pink, red and blue gels so you can change the color of the spot if you want to. But most of the time, you probably will use a white or flesh pink color. You'll be able to create a mood with the colored gels in the other lights. Use the follow spot to keep the audience's attention on you throughout the show regardless of any other changes in lighting.

The next thing to bring in is two light "trees," one for each side of the stage. Each "tree" should have at least five Fresnels* on it, two red, two blue, and one amber. Fresnels are fixed spot lights used primarily to effect color changes. These light "trees," so named because they stand freely and have metal "branches" on which lights are hung, provide an excellent, inexpensive and varied source of *side* lighting. They are essential to the other important function of lighting—creating a mood. If you're singing a ballad, use the blue Fresnels to bathe the stage in blue light. If you're doing an up-tempo song, use the red Fresnels to bathe the stage in red. Use the amber Fresnels for a shuffle

* pronounced Fruh - *nel*.

# LIGHTING ILLUSTRATION

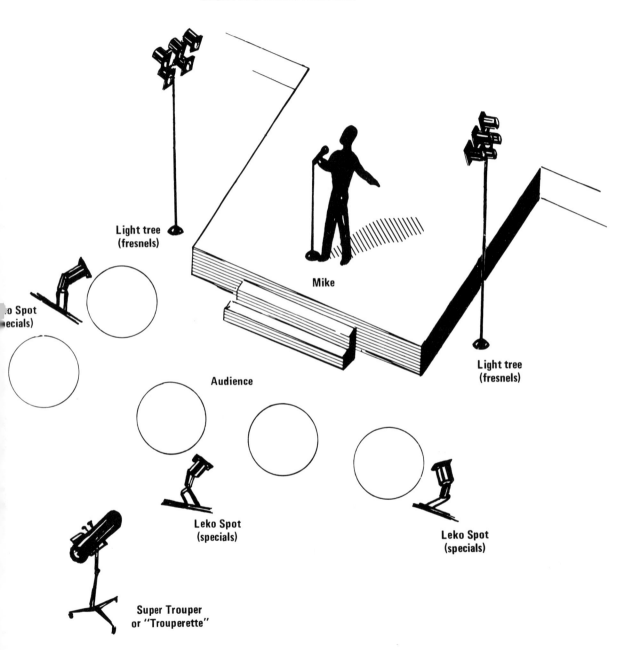

Light tree
(fresnels)

Mike

Leko Spot
(specials)

Audience

Light tree
(fresnels)

Leko Spot
(specials)

Leko Spot
(specials)

Super Trouper
or "Trouperette"

rhythm, a country song or any song with a medium tempo. With a Trouperette follow spot and these two light "trees," you have the fundamental components of theatrical lighting. You have lighting to focus the audience's attention—the follow spot light—and you have lighting to create a mood—the light "trees."

Lighting also should provide *visual variety,* however, and since three colors in side lighting and one follow spot are capable of providing only so much variety, you now should add two or three fixed Leko spot lights, called "specials," in front of the stage. These should be mounted to or hung from the ceiling out in front of the proscenium (or the edge of the stage if there is no proscenium). In other words, they are high, *front* lighting. One of the Leko "specials" should be focused so that it creates a pool of light on the stage which you can step into for effect. The other two "specials" should be shuttered so that they provide a *wash* of light on each side of the stage.

The follow spot requires an operator. But the light "trees" and the "specials" can be operated from the stage with a series of foot switches. If you have another volunteer and a dimmer board for these lights, the effects you can create by fading in and out of different colors and lights sources can be spectacular. And these lighting components should not be unreasonably expensive. Often, they can be rented for the length of your engagement from a local theatrical lighting company. Look in the Yellow Pages. Ask the management of the club where you're working to absorb the cost and, if they refuse, spend the money yourself. You never will be able to perform successfully as a singing entertainer if you don't have the benefit of basic show lighting.

One final note about lighting. Keep in mind that the audience will focus its attention wherever you focus light. Thus, you shouldn't light the band, except subtly, unless there is a specific reason for doing so. The purpose of lighting is to focus the audience's attention on you.


## WARDROBE

This is the Glitter Era. In the large supper clubs around the country, and in the showrooms of Las Vegas, Reno and Tahoe, performers are

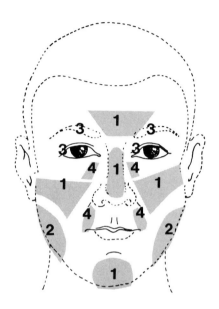

## MAN'S MAKE-UP ILLUSTRATION

### General
All make-up should be water resistant and dry—not greasy
All tones should be blended
No lipstick

### Specific
1 — Dark Rouge—Bronzer to give sun-tanned healthy look
2 — Hollow cheeks—dark tone
3 — Mascara on eye lashes and eye brows
4 — White or "erase" to take away dark creases and/or
     diminish wrinkles

wearing tuxedos or custom-made outfits elaborately decorated with sequins, embroidery and beads. Until you start playing those rooms, you don't need anything that fancy. Your stage clothes should be chosen to suit the occasion. Let's be honest, a sequined tuxedo on stage at the Holiday Inn in Duluth is a bit much. Dress for the room. Pay attention to current fashion styles and reflect those styles on stage, but only if they are flattering to you. What you wear on stage should be "stageworthy." In other words, your clothes should be clean, neatly pressed, well-fitting, flattering and appropriate.

Have fun with your wardrobe. You should look comfortable and feel comfortable in what you wear. After all, the purpose of stage clothes is to make you as attractive and appealing as possible. If your wardrobe fills this purpose, you're ready to go on stage.

## MAKE-UP

Women generally know how to apply make-up and, if they don't, they can seek the advice and assistance of other women. Men, on the other hand, usually are uninitiated when it comes to make-up and, therefore, think they don't need it. Hence, what follows are some stage make-up hints for men. The purpose of stage make-up, for men or women, is to make you appear more attractive and healthy and put back some of the facial definition which is obliterated by harsh stage lighting. Without make-up, a man's face, like a woman's, will appear "washed out," pale. With the application of relatively small amounts of natural-looking make-up, however, a man can appear to be healthy, sun-tanned and yet masculine while in the glare of stage lights.

The secret to any good make-up job lies in the type of make-up used and in the method of application. Men never should use "pancake" make-up, that is, a thick base which covers the face completely. However, men may use modest amounts of eyebrow pencil and eye-liner to accentuate their eyes, and they may apply skin toner (bronzing lotion) and rouge to accentuate cheek bones and make the complexion appear ruddy. If applied properly, this type of make-up is difficult to detect, even up close, and yet it does a great deal to enhance your appearance on stage.

If you wear make-up on stage, remember that you also must make-up your *hands*. For if you don't, when you are holding the microphone up to your mouth, your hands will appear pale in contrast to your face. This is a dead giveaway that you are wearing facial make-up. Apply the same skin toner to your hands as you have applied to your face, then stand in front of a mirror and hold your hands up to your face and see if they "match."

## PRODUCER'S CHECK-LIST

In the formative stages of your career when you are assembling your stage act, you must be, in every sense, your own producer. As such, you must be the catalyst for the creation and execution of all the various elements in your act. The time will come, of course, when you must take off your producer's hat and put on your performer's hat. But, for the time being, your job is to conceive and plan a stageworthy show. As you face this formidable task, you may find it useful from time to time to review the following check-list:

1. Do you know who you want to be on stage? Have you explored and chosen the attitudes which will make up your performing, "public self?" According to our singer's survey, 42% of the performers who responded said that, on stage, they feel they are exactly the same person they are off-stage. 33% said they are basically themselves on stage but that they adopt a "public posture or attitude." And 25% said that, on-stage, they are playing a role, "much as an actor plays a role," which is *unlike* who they are off-stage.
2. Have you chosen songs which are good vehicles for your particular talents? Does the material in your act say who you are as an individual?

3. Have you developed concepts for medleys which are interesting and which will give your show added texture and dimension? Do these concepts relate to and reinforce who you are, how you want to be seen?

4. Are your concepts for audience participation feasible and, more importantly, will you feel comfortable executing them? Have you taken into account all the possible variables?

5. Is there a purpose for everything you plan to do on stage? Will your act *flow* naturally from one point to the next?

6. Do you have enough material to fill 30 minutes? If so, will you have enough to fill 45 minutes, if necessary?

7. Are you *technically* prepared to perform? Have you made allowances for wardrobe and make-up? Have you made arrangements for lighting and planned how your show will be lit? Have you arranged for a sound system? If so, are you sure it will be adequate in every respect?

8. Have you set up rehearsal times with your musical director? With your musicians? Have you allowed time for a technical (lighting and sound) rehearsal of your show?

9. Are you emotionally and physically prepared to perform? Are you healthy and well-rested? Are you in good voice?

10. Have you planned what you are going to *say* on stage?

# CHAPTER 5

# "BLAH, BLAH, BLAH"

*"Speech is civilization itself. The word,*
*even the most contradictory word, preserves*
*contact—it is silence which isolates."*
— *Thomas Mann*

**You're in your garage** or you've rented a rehearsal hall, and you're ready to run through your act. You've picked all the songs, routined them with your musical director or pianist and rehearsed them with your band.

You've got a strong opening song (an "opener"), a well-paced set of songs which make up the body of your show, and you have a good, strong closing number (a "closer"). Musically, the show seems right.

You've thought about how you are going to make your entrance and your exit. You've planned how you are going to move on stage—perhaps you'll sit on a stool for a ballad, perhaps you have choreographed some dance steps to do during a disco or rock song.

You think you're ready.

The band starts to play. You make your entrance at the appropriate time after the overture or during the "play on." And you sing your first song. It goes well.

When you finish the song, you turn to the band and your musical director and say, ". . . And then I say, 'blah, blah, blah' and we go into the second song."

103

Someone counts off the next song, and you continue running through your act. You've just made one of the most serious—and most common—mistakes which inexperienced singers make. You've practiced everything else—your entrance, your stage movements, your exit. You've rehearsed the words you're going to *sing*. But you haven't rehearsed the words you're going to *speak*.

Dissolve.

Now, you're on stage. You're in the middle of your act. The band sounds fine. You sound fine. The songs are fine. But, in between songs, you have nothing to say. You simply sing song after song. Or you talk, but your talk is rambling or too long. You thought you knew what you wanted to say, but now it has no real structure. It's haphazard. You're relying on spontaneity. You reach for something humorous and it misses. You can't seem to establish any rapport with the audience.

Maybe you've been there. Or maybe you've seen other performers in this predicament. It's painful, sometimes. Some performers babble on about nothing in particular, without being amusing, desperately trying to fill the "dead air" between songs.

Don't let this happen to you.

Just saying "blah, blah, blah" in rehearsal is not enough. You must plan, write and rehearse what you're actually going to say on stage. For talking is as important as singing to a singing entertainer.

You must communicate totally in order to entertain totally. And to communicate totally, you must *talk*. In our daily lives, we don't sing to one another, we speak. Speaking reveals who we are.

As a performer, you reveal who you are when you talk. You give the audience an idea of what you are really like as a person and allow them to see another dimension of your personality. What you say, as much as what you sing, is what makes an audience care about you. And until an audience cares, you'll never be able to move them with what you sing.

Every successful singing entertainer will tell you it is essential to be able to talk effectively on stage. You must give the audience a chance to become involved in what you do. In his book, "Yes I Can," Sammy Davis, Jr. says he realized early in his career that it didn't matter how he sang or what he sang if the audience didn't have empathy for him as a person. In recent years, many singers have begun to place much more emphasis on talking to their audiences. For they have come to realize that their artistic strengths are enhanced by developing greater personal rapport. Unlike the classical singer or opera singer or the singer in a musical production, the pop singer—the person behind the voice—must come forward and take responsibility for creating a relationship with the audience.

## REASONS FOR TALKING ON STAGE

Consider the practical reasons why the singing entertainer talks:

First, to welcome the audience to the showplace and, in that welcome, to make them feel comfortable and a part of the show. If you ignore the importance of a basic greeting at the outset of the show, the audience will feel alienated both from you as a performer and from your performance. Until you, the singer, reach out to include them, they are relegated to being observers. Observers might make a good television or movie audience, but they don't make a very good nightclub or concert audience.

Second, to make the audience laugh. Humor is one of the most attractive and disarming tools a performer can use. Laughter breaks down barriers—it makes people feel less inhibited. Once the audience is laughing, they are more accessible. If you can reach an audience with humor, you can win them.

You already should know the value of humor on stage from your own personal experiences off stage. When you meet someone who is humorous—not obnoxious, but witty and charming—you immediately feel more at ease. The same dynamic exists between an audience and a performer. When you come on stage, the audience is meeting you, perhaps for the first time. As the performer, you automatically have an elevated position, physically and psychologically. The audience, therefore, has certain natural fears. They fear you may be intimidating rather than accommodating. They fear you may be pompous and aloof. They fear you won't let them "in." Yet, if you—like the charming and witty stranger—reveal you have a sense of humor about yourself and are capable of laughing with the audience and getting them to laugh with you, they will feel at ease with you.

Third, to set up the next song (or medley) and let the audience know how you want them to respond. By talking, the singing entertainer can, to a large extent, manage audience reaction. If you simply sing song after song, without stopping to include the audience in the design of your show, they will become lost and never know exactly how they are expected to react.

Fourth, to develop audience participation. At some point in the show, a singing entertainer should have material which enables him or her to go into the audience, or bring people to the stage, or otherwise get people directly involved in the performance.

Fifth, to introduce the band and/or the orchestra. A singing entertainer briefly introduces and thanks those who make the show happen— musicians, singers and dancers—as a courtesy. And by doing so, the performer demonstrates that he is also a courteous person.

Sixth, and finally, to say goodnight and thank the audience. As you would if you have spent an evening at a friend's house, you must finally announce your departure and thank the audience for their attention and approval.

Whenever you talk on stage, you should have one of the above purposes for speaking in mind.


## YOUR OPENING TALK

Your welcome or opening talk should not come until you have established yourself as a singer. To use the analogy of entertaining at home again, you should act as if you are welcoming friends to an intimate party.

Here are some specific suggestions for opening talks:

Talk about the time of day of the show and how it feels to perform at this time. If it's Tuesday night, you might say, "It's Tuesday night and a lot of people think nothing ever happens on Tuesday night. I love

Tuesday nights, though, because when it's Tuesday you know Friday is only *three* days away!" Watch "The Tonight Show" and you will notice that the host often refers to the audience he had the night before. "You seem like a great audience," he will say, "but last night we had a mean crowd . . . etc."

You might want to talk about what you think certain individuals in the audience would be doing if they weren't attending tonight's performance. You can tailor your opening remarks to fit a particular town—talk about local problems which are humorous and affect the audience or compare the city you're currently working in to other cities where you've performed. Be careful, however, not to alienate your audience by being too sarcastic or flippant about local traditions or customs. Sometimes, localized humor can backfire. So, if you have an idea, check it out with people who live in the area.

You may be able to develop an opening talk by observing certain peculiarities about the audience—the type of cars in the parking lot; the ratio of men to women in the audience; the way members of the audience are dressed; the number of soft drinks sold or the amount of alcohol consumed before the show started; the number of people wearing glasses. Being observant lets the audience know you're aware of them and appreciate them as a group, and your observations can tell you a lot about what kind of crowd they will be.

Consider topics like these for opening stories: How you got to the show tonight; trying to buy shoes to match your suit; how the Mayor welcomed you to the city; how your brother talked you into going into show business; how you got rid of the girls in your dressing room so you could do the show; how it's not easy to sing after having the dinner you just had. You might create a story about how a man had a fight with his wife during your last show, or make up a funny story about the history of the theater (or club) where you're working—little-known facts about the architecture, the name and location.

Your opening talk will be strongest and score the best if it is built in some way around your audience. The more you talk about them, so long as you use good taste and do it in fun, the better they will like it. Again, it is analagous to having people to your house—if you talk about them, show a concern for them, then they will enjoy the evening more. More importantly, they will know that you care about them and be more likely to care about you. Whatever you do, don't go on and on about yourself. The purpose of your opening talk is to extend a welcoming hand to the audience and make them comfortable in your domain.


## COMEDY SPOTS

Comedy will do more to relax an audience than practially anything else you can do. But remember you're a singer, not a comedian. People don't expect you to be Rodney Dangerfield or Henny Youngman, so don't approach joke-telling or story-telling the way they do. Most singers who use comedy material appear to enjoy the jokes as much as the audience does, as if they are hearing the jokes for the first time. A singer is better off laughing at his own jokes—it makes him more human. Norm Crosby, Jerry Van Dyke and Red Skelton are good examples of comedians who laugh at their own jokes and they are, therefore, good examples for singers to study. The dead-pan delivery which made Jack Benny a legend, on the other hand, would not work well for most singers. It would appear too cold and calculated; it would seem like you're working too hard for the laughs. If you enjoy your jokes right along with the audience, your comedy will appear to be secondary to your main purpose—singing—and it will be all the more engaging.

Don't rely on being funny on the spur of the moment on stage. You should use only those jokes and stories which you have tested and learned. You should know that the material you're going to do is funny and will work. Now, you may be thinking, this all sounds too premeditated, too planned. But that is exactly how successful comedy is performed. Any comedy writer will tell you, comedy is *serious* business. The best comedians always know what they're going to do—they meticulously plan their material. You may think they're "winging it," but more often than not they've used the very same gags many times before.

Your delivery is what makes the joke appear to be spontaneous. The audience shouldn't know you're telling a joke until it's too late and they're laughing. Then, it doesn't matter if they realize it was a joke, that you planned it and didn't just make it up. Once you have several jokes and stories in your show which work, you must make a conscious effort each time you tell them to invest new enthusiasm and conviction in them. Don't let a joke get tired. If you get tired of it and throw away the delivery, you're throwing away the joke.

If you buy jokes from comedy writers, try to make a deal whereby you only have to pay for the jokes you use. Some writers will not work on this basis. They will charge a flat fee for a certain number of jokes or for so many minutes of comedy material. If the material doesn't work, you've wasted your money, and you probably won't go back to that writer in the future. Tell the comedy writer you will pay for what you use and you will buy as many jokes as he or she can write, so long as they work for you. This arrangement actually works out better for both the singer and the writer: the singer gets what he needs and the writer gets repeat business.


## SETTING UP SONGS

To be an effective singing entertainer, you must lead the audience through your show. Let the audience know what you're going to do before you do it. They will be able to follow you better and, consequently, will respond more favorably. This is done by including short talk spots—set ups—before certain songs, medleys or audience participation segments.

For example, you might say, "I'm going to sing for you my choices for the best love songs from this past year. See if you don't agree these are the songs that will be remembered from this year." You have sign-posted what you're about to do—you've said you're going to do love songs; you've said you're going to do the best love songs, which implies a medley; and you've asked the audience to agree with your choices. The audience knows what you expect of them. If they recognize the songs, they probably will applaud at the beginning of each song. They will give you approval *if* you ask for it. And when the medley is over, they will know you want their reaction. They also will expect you to move on and take them with you.

Lead the audience from moment to moment in the show. Never shock them, unless you deliberately do so for effect. As a singing entertainer you are host, master of ceremonies and tour guide as well as singer.

Set-ups to songs or musical segments also can be used to help create a mood. What you say gets the audience on your "wave length" and lets them know how you feel. Often, a mood can be created without talking specifically about the song you're going to sing. A set-up never should be so elaborate that it makes the song which follows seem anti-climactic.

## AUDIENCE PARTICIPATION

If there's a place in your act where you want the audience to participate, you will need a certain amount of *prepared* talk to get into and out of the segment.

Diana Ross, for example, involves her audience in singing a song called "Reach Out And Touch." She begins by sitting down on the edge of the stage and telling the audience that this is her favorite song, one she has sung for many years. She sets a very intimate mood. (The show up to this point usually is dazzling with slick production.) Then she moves into the audience singing "Reach out and touch/Somebody's hand/Make this world a better place/If you can."[1] But she isn't finished talking, yet. She continues, as she moves from table to table and from

[1]"Reach Out and Touch" by Nickolas Ashford and Valerie Simpson © 1970, Jobete Music Co., Inc. (ASCAP)

person to person, to develop the idea of togetherness. She selects several people to sing with her as the band continues to play. She gets all the ladies to sing; then she gets all the men to sing.

Throughout this audience participation segment, Diana Ross' talk promotes the purpose of the segment—to bridge the gap between her and the audience and to spread a feeling of warmth, closeness and caring. She skillfully succeeds on both counts, and the result is an out-pouring of affection for Diana and a feeling that she has reached out and touched us as we have touched her.

Talk spots which go along with audience participation numbers are perhaps the most difficult to write because they must be simple, informal, direct, instructive and still leave you some room to deal with the unexpected. You have to remember where you're going, but you also must be prepared and loose enough to *ad lib* when necessary. You've got to be able to think on your feet and react quickly.

## THANK YOU'S

When thanking the band and/or orchestra, remember the audience rarely cares about those in the background. Their attention and affection is focused on the singer, the "star." They came to see you and, unless one of your musicians, singers or dancers is a celebrity in his or her own right, they have no reason to be interested in anyone except you. Nevertheless, recognition is important to everyone, and your musicians (singers, dancers, etc.) would be offended—and rightfully so—if you did not introduce them and thank them publicly. It's also a long-standing tradition in show business to do this and a gracious thing for the "star" to do. But, if you forget to introduce your band, the majority of the people in the audience probably won't notice. They simply don't care.

So, make your introductions and thank-you's of the band short and to the point. Inside jokes between you and members of your group on stage are self-indulgent and make the audience feel left out. Everything you say or do on stage should be audience-oriented.

## GOOD NIGHTS

Your "good-bye" or "good-night" at the end of a show should be said simply and sincerely. You should know exactly when you're going to say "good-bye," thank the audience warmly, then get off. The only reason to linger for a moment, once you've said "thank you" and "good-bye," is to appreciate the audience's applause. Let them know you *hear* and appreciate their reaction. Then go. Be decisive. You must end a show as definitely as you began. You must tell the audience in so many words, "This is the end."

Of course, if an encore is warranted, you may return to the stage. Say something which lets the audience know how much you appreciate the fact that they want more. You might also wish to say something humorous. To let the audience know that you are accustomed to doing an encore, you could say after you return to the stage, "That's a little game I play . . . called 'Go back and touch the wall . . .' " as Kenny Rogers does. Or, if the audience gives you a standing ovation, you could say, "Thank you for standing up . . . I know you were just leaving, but I appreciate it anyway!"

## CENSORING YOURSELF

A few words about good taste. Let's say someone asks you to sing for a group of teenagers or children. Should you tell the same jokes and sing the same suggestive songs you sing for adults? First of all, people under the age of 13—children—generally aren't going to understand sophisticated material or suggestive jokes and songs. Secondly, teenagers generally know more about sex these days than most adults. They won't be offended, though sometimes their parents will take offense on their behalf. Finally, you shouldn't be doing material which is tasteless, vulgar or offensive in front of either adults, teenagers or children. If a song or joke is merely risque or tastefully erotic and basically inoffensive, any contemporary person will enjoy it. The people who would take offense are not the people who usually go to popular concerts, nightclubs and lounges or otherwise support the pop music industry.


## COLLECTING MATERIAL

How do you find material to talk about on stage?

Perhaps the best way to begin is by keeping a notebook or file of ideas for "talk spots." Remember anecdotes you hear and write them down; then try to put yourself in the story to see if it's something you can say happened to you. Keep notes about your personal experiences; work them up into short, amusing statements which can be related to a song or musical segment. Write down jokes you hear. Read joke books. You can learn a lot about what makes jokes funny by reading a lot of jokes. Study the forms of jokes—some jokes involve a play on words, some involve an unexpected twist of logic, some involve absurdity or exaggeration.

Keep a catalogue, by subject, of comedy segments and jokes. This accomplishes a number of things. It enables you to store material you currently are not using and retrieve that material when you wish to use it again. A comedy file also allows you to find material quickly for special occasions. And having a collection of material gives you the freedom to mix-and-match jokes and segments so that your act always appears to be fresh.


## BASIC RULES

When you are planning the talk set-ups for your act, remember these points:

1. Don't talk about yourself; talk about the audience, the songs or what you want the audience to do. It's okay to talk about how you feel occasionally, if it helps to set a mood.

2. Don't talk before every song; let musical transitions, lighting changes or changes in your attitude or energy provide the set-up for a bridge between some songs. Don't underestimate the element of surprise. Sometimes it is more effective to simply begin the song and let the audience discover it with you.

3. Don't explain every song; let the audience use its imagination. If you make your explanation of the meaning of a song too detailed, you leave no room for individual interpretation. John Denver has said that he never explains the *meaning* of his songs to an audience. As a result, he has found that different songs hold different meanings for different people. Joe Brooks' "You Light Up My Life," the Debby Boone hit, is a good example of a song which you should allow the audience to interpret. Some people think "You Light Up My Life" is about God; in other words, they wish to choose the religious interpretation. Others prefer the more obvious love song interpretation; in other words, the song is about two people in love. In most cases, your songs will be received better if you let people supply the meaning the song has for them.

4. Whenever you talk to the audience, do it as though you are talking to *one* person. Too many entertainers make the mistake of using a loud, public, oratorial type voice to address the audience; it's as if they are giving a political speech. It's cold and impersonal. Your talk should be *conversational*. Avoid using phrases like "Ladies and Gentlemen" or "My friends." Address the audience as you would a friend or an acquaintance, as "you." Practice speaking into your tape recorder. Imagine you're in front of thousands of people. You must communicate in clear, straight forward terms. But speak as though you're talking to one person, as though you're confiding in a friend on a personal level. After all, you want the audience to be your friend, so relate to them that way.

## TV TALK SHOWS

Except for on stage, the place where the singer's ability to talk, be charming and funny is most important is on television talk shows.

Most television talk shows are not really *talk* shows—they are *entertainment* shows. That is, the popularity and success of the show is based on its entertainment value. Whatever the guests say has to be entertaining. That's the yardstick by which everything said on a talk show is measured.

"The Tonight Show" is a prime example of an entertainment-talk show. After the talent coordinators and the producer select who is going to be on the show (called "booking" the show), each guest is contacted in advance, usually by telephone, by a coordinator or writer who conducts a pre-interview of the guest.

The primary purpose of the pre-interview is to find out what topics of conversation will make the guest most entertaining on the show. The coordinator or writer will discuss topics with the guest which he or she thinks the audience will find interesting and, hopefully, funny. The coordinator or writer will discourage the guest from talking about certain subjects, such as the guest's favorite charities, new mansion in Beverly Hills or opinions on weighty and complicated issues. Usually, the pre-interviewer also tries to keep the guest from talking only about his latest film, record or TV series. The latter is called "plugging" and, generally, the TV audience isn't interested in listening to a celebrity drone on about his latest product.

Virtually everything a guest says or does on "The Tonight Show" or on any of the other entertainment-talk shows, has been discussed, planned and agreed upon in a pre-interview. The job of the coordinator or writer is to make the show entertaining. And the only way to make it entertaining is to select the most interesting and humorous anecdotes, stories and topics from each guest. If a celebrity has a funny story about getting trapped in an elevator, then the pre-interviewer writes a question for the host to ask which will lead the guest into the story. The host might say, "I understand you just finished a tour. Did you have any problems on the road?" The guest then will explain that the tour went well, but there was a funny thing that happened in Toledo . . . in an elevator. If the questions are well-written and the stories they set-up are, indeed, funny, then the interview goes well. It appears to be natural and spontaneous, and it's entertaining.

Talk shows don't like to take risks. It's dangerous to hope that a guest will be interesting, amusing or funny. Some of the biggest stars are notoriously boring when they sit and talk, unless they are given something to talk about or led into telling their best stories.

Now that you know that talk shows are thoroughly premeditated, you can watch them from a different perspective. Notice how questions asked of comics when they're sitting at the "panel" (i.e., on the couch) with the host or hostess invariably set-up jokes. This is called "sit-down" comedy. When a comedian does one of the talk shows, he usually needs enough material to do 3-5 minutes standing up and 2 to 3 minutes sitting down.

A singer on a TV talk show usually will be guaranteed time to do only one song. A good rule of thumb is to make your first song up-tempo, familiar and contemporary. If you have a chance to do a second song, you could do something original or unfamiliar, but make sure it is powerful comedically or dramatically and a proven audience-pleaser. After your song, you *may* be asked to join the host or hostess at the "panel" to talk. If so, this is the part of your appearance which must be well-planned in the pre-interview. Keep in mind that TV talk shows frequently are wary of singers as guests because, all too often, they have nothing interesting to say; unlike comics, they have no prepared material which will entertain and get laughs. Thus, the more material you can develop and suggest to the talk show pre-interviewer, the better.

Some good things to prepare are: Comedy songs which you can do simply while sitting at the "panel"; funny stories of various types; an exciting instrumental performance, such as on banjo or fiddle; or something you can demonstrate or teach the host how to do (called a "demo").

In short, figure out what will make you a desirable guest. Again, as in entertaining any audience, you must do more than sing. You must be as successful as a personality as you are as a performer. Watch entertainment-talk shows: "The Tonight Show," "Merv Griffin," "Dinah!" and "The Mike Douglas Show." Basically, if you can score on any one of these shows, you can score on them all.

("The Phil Donahue Show" and Dick Cavett's current show on PBS—public television—are essentialy *talk-only* shows. They are in the tradition of the old "David Frost Show" from New York and have formats which allow you to just sit around and talk without having to be funny. In fact, Phil Donahue typically has only one guest on each show and often deals with one subject. But his in-depth style of interviewing and lack of emphasis on entertainment per se is the exception, not the rule.)

Some information on how to audition and submit yourself for TV entertainment-talk shows follows in Chapter Nine. But before you worry about getting on one of these shows, be sure you're prepared. If you bomb, chances are it'll be a long time before they ask you back.

Spend your time writing, collecting, perhaps buying, and working out various kinds of material for your act—stories, jokes, comedy songs, set-ups for songs, musical segments and so on. That's the first priority. While you're in the process of doing that, you can put aside certain pieces of material which you feel might be suitable for TV. And when the time comes, you'll have a number of ideas to discuss with that talent coordinator or writer from your favorite TV talk show—the one that wants to book you.

Whatever you do, keep developing as a versatile singing entertainer. That will do more to get you on television than anything else. The television shows, whether variety or entertainment-talk, prefer to book singers who already have achieved some degree of notariety or celebrity status. And the people who produce and book these shows must believe you will add entertainment value. There has to be a hook on which they can hang your booking. Maybe you're the hottest singer in Columbus, Ohio or Detroit, Michigan. Maybe you're the only nuclear physicist who ever became a pop singer. Maybe you've had a Top 10 record and broken through that way.

## TOTAL COMMUNICATION

In conclusion, in order to become a total entertainer, you must be able to communicate totally. The ability to be yourself when you are talking on stage, the ability to be interesting and humorous, and the ability to communicate intimately with a large audience are as important as the ability to sing perfect tones. In fact, these qualities are essential. If you should neglect their development, one day it might be said that you are an exciting singer but, when you talk, you are "blah, blah, blah."

JOHN DAVIDSON'S SINGERS' SUMMER CAMP

CATALINA ISLAND

A

# A Letter From John

Dear JDSSC Applicant,

First of all, thank you for your interest in JDSSC. This Summer Program is a dream come true for me and I hope it will be the same for you. This experience, this workshop, has never before been offered anywhere in the world and I am convinced that if you make full use of our program, your chances for a successful career in show business will be greatly improved.

Your four weeks at JDSSC should accomplish several goals:

1. Our approach should save you time and money, especially in the early stages of your career.

2. We will expand the scope of your career, as well as your talents by introducing you to all styles of popular music.

3. You will be surrounded by other performers, like yourself, who are striving for the same objectives and this will provide a forum for an exchange of contemporary musical ideas.

4. We will illustrate to you that popular singing, in its most commercial form, is art with its own rules and formulas that require dedication and discipline.

5. We will help you to enhance the 'tools of your trade':
   Sight Singing, Dance, Comedy, Choosing and tailor-making material for yourself and Voice Production.

6. Through practical experience in front of an audience which represents a cross-section of America, you will know immediately which material 'works'.

Now, our Program may not be right for you or vice versa. Let me explain. We are looking for young performers between the ages of 18 and 30 who want to become better singing entertainers. These are not singers who just sing. We want you to come to JDSSC with the intention of entertaining people with music through the use of comedy songs, medleys and 'audience bits'. We will encourage you to use well-known contemporary material. We want you to perform in your own style, but we insist that you move the audience to laughter or tears or touch them in some way. Naturally, the more experience in live performance you have had, the quicker and easier you will benefit from our Program. In short, we want to develop dynamic, well-rounded entertainers who can succeed on television, on records and in live performances. With this kind of training, your career can take on lifetime proportions.

I will personally be at the Camp for three weeks of each Session and will be critiqueing the performances each weekend at the Avalon Bowl. I will be lecturing during the first week in the evening seminars and during the following weeks we will have guest speakers from the entertainment world live and on video tape.

If you feel you would benefit from sharing your talents with us and ours with you, I will look forward to working with you this Summer on Catalina Island.

Sincerely,

B

# COURSES OF STUDY

**SIGHT SINGING**

One-hour group classes Monday through Wednesday mornings. These sessions are divided into basic and intermediate. Students will become familiar with relative pitch and rhythmic values to enable them to sing a piece of music that they have never seen nor heard before.

**DANCE CLASS**

One-hour group classes twice a week in jazz, tap and soft-shoe, as well as contemporary styles. Emphasis is on movement while singing, not featured dance solos.

**PRIVATE SESSIONS WITH ARRANGERS**

Each student will work one hour each day with his arranger. Time will be spent choosing material, laying out medleys and musical segments, and basic vocal coaching. In these sessions, two pieces of material will be chosen and rehearsed for the weekend performances at the Avalon Bowl. Your arranger will be accompanying you on an electric piano.

**MORNING WORKSHOP**

One-hour session Monday through Thursday mornings. There will be four different speakers, one each week, lecturing on (1) Comedy; (2) Musical drama; (3) The business of show business; (4) Preparation of material. All of our speakers are professionals in their fields and have had practical experiences in show business.

**DRAMATIC INTERPRETATION**

Group class three one-hour sessions per week. In order to improve the dramatic approach to a song, we will study Shakespearean sonnets and perform them as dramatic interpretations. Sonnets are 14 lines, have musical rhythm, and contain metaphors and verbal images which resemble popular songs.

**EVENING SEMINARS**

Two-hour sessions after dinner Monday through Wednesday. Guest speakers will share their experiences with us. In past seasons our guest speakers have been John Davidson, Kenny Rogers, Florence Hendersen, Shields & Yarnell, Andy Williams, Pete Barbutti, Jim Teeter, and Pierre Cossette, as well as agents, managers, television producers and musical directors.

**PRIVATE VOCAL INSTRUCTION**

One-half hour lesson as needed. For those students who are interested in improving their vocal production, we offer private voice lessons taught by a professional voice teacher. Not a required course.

**LIVE PERFORMANCE**

Each weekend each student will perform two pieces of material at the Avalon Bowl. This material will be created and rehearsed in the private arranging sessions. Singers will sing with a four-piece group consisting of piano, guitar, bass and drums. There are five shows each weekend featuring approximately ten singers per show. Show Times: Friday 4:30, Saturday 2:00 and 4:30, Sunday 2:00 and 4:30. We will record these performances on cassette and on video tape for educational purposes. Your arrangements and audio tapes are yours to take with you.

*All specifics regarding JDSSC are subject to change in future sessions.*

C

Dance Class

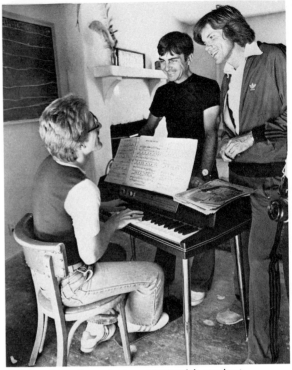

John observing private session with student and arranger.

Sight Reading Class

Avalon Bowl

D

# FACILITIES

## ACCOMMODATIONS

JDSSC is located on Catalina Island, which is 30 miles off the coast of California. We are nestled in Toyon Bay, which is 20 minutes by shore boat from Avalon. Because of its location and our limited facility, we do not allow visitors on Campus. All rooms are singles; all bedding is supplied except towels. There are dorms for the Men and the Women with the lavatories at the end of each hall. We recommend bringing a bathrobe. The commissary is cafeteria style, and the Campus Store supplies us with soft drinks, candy, peanuts, etc. We have coin-operated laundry rooms with washers and dryers. Although the brochure looks very beautiful, you should be aware that this is a Summer **Camp.** Ours is a natural, rustic setting, with **extremely** simple accommodations. I feel that the facilities are ideal for our needs. We have plenty of rehearsal rooms, large meeting halls for our evening seminars and private listening alcoves for music study in the library.

## LIBRARIES

We have an extensive collection of books pertaining to voice, comedy and show business. Our record album and sheet music files are quite complete and are augmented whenever necessary.

## RECREATION

We offer tennis, softball, basketball, volleyball, swimming, snorkeling in the ocean and miles of secluded hiking trails.

## WHAT TO BRING

You will need to bring the following:

1) Your own personal towels; 2) An inexpensive cassette recorder and ten one-hour cassettes; 3) All sheet music or small arrangements, if you have them, for piano, bass, drums and guitar, that you presently have been working on; 4) Any instruments that you use on stage; 5) Personal spending money for free time in Avalon, tennis racket and tennis balls, sneakers, diving mask, fins and snorkel, flashlight, and hiking boots, if desired.

## PERSONAL CLOTHING

Our Campus is located on the Ocean. The days are hot and the nights are cooler, so we recommend a sweater. All clothes are casual, such as shorts, jeans. T-shirts The only dressy clothes you'll need are for your performances at the Avalon Bowl. For these performances, each student will need four outfits. All performances are outside in the daytime. We would like the ladies to perform in casual summer dresses and the men to wear sport shirts and slacks or neat and clean jeans.

E

An evening seminar with John.

Guest Speakers

Florence Henderson

F

Kenny Rogers

Informal get together offers a chance to share ideas.

Guest speaker—
Andy Williams

G

The following excerpts are from leading magazines, newspapers and trade papers such as Variety, Newsweek, Billboard, The Washington Post and many others.

# Newspaper Clippings

## A Workshop for Warblers

— Newsweek

The thing you have to remember all the way through is compromise," explains the camp's introductory lecturer. "You have to tailor your act so it's commercially acceptable. I don't think you should write a totally original act. Give in to public requests and demands. Sing what is on the charts. It is not so bad."

He needn't worry. The 50 fresh-faced students before him would gladly trade originality for secure careers as the warbling lounge singers and supper-club thrushes of tomorrow. "I've played every Holiday Inn, Sheraton and Marriott on the East Coast as a warm-up act," explains 21-year-old Toni Taylor from Pittsburgh. "I'd be happy to go back if I could just have my own act. This camp can work for me. You say you went to John Davidson, and agents know your act has been packaged by professionals."

It is the first of two four-week sessions at John Davidson's Singers' Summer Camp, a nonprofit school for would-be nightclub entertainers who want to pattern themselves after the camp's middle-of-the-road musical namesake. John Davidson neither writes his own songs nor sells many records. Nonetheless, he will earn $2 million this year in nightclub appearances, stylizing the songs of others. "He's got his thing down," says camp musical director Billy Fellows. "John jumps and leaps around and hugs the ladies. He's an entertainer."

**Homogeneous:** For Davidson, the camp represents the consummation of a five-year dream. "There are other music camps," he says, "but none that treats pop singing as an art form." Students pay $1,600 to learn singing, tap and soft-shoe dancing, sight reading, showmanship and "audience rapport." Following 7 a.m. calisthenics and a jog around the campgrounds on Catalina Island, off Los Angeles, the all-day round of classes is conducted by Davidson, six vocal coaches and such guest instructors as Andy Williams, Kenny Rogers and Ed McMahon.

The teachers have their work cut out for them. Of the 470 applicants who sent in the required voice tapes and photographs, nearly half sang "Feelings" — an outpouring so blandly homogeneous Davidson himself was appalled. Even among the 50 campers chosen for the first session, so many patterned themselves after their heroes that vocal coach John Toben quipped: "We've come to Barry Manilow, not to praise him." Debbie Lesser, 20, of Cleveland, says her ambition is "to be a backup singer and dancer for Juliet Prowse or Lola Falana." Echoes Cindy Carmody, 20, who has played in the 747 Lounge in Taylor, Mich., and at the Pampa Lanes bowling alley in East Detroit: "I'd like to have the same amount of say that Vikki Carr has. I want my own orchestra."

To help out the songbirds, Davidson and his guest lecturers offer up bits of professional advice: study performers on TV variety shoes; avoid cocktail parties (they induce vocal fatigue); hold the microphone loosely, as you might an ice-cream sandwich. Several of the male campers had to be admonished not to prance about with limp wrists: "It detracts from your credibility when you smooch up to the women at the tables."

**Hired Entertainment:** Most important are the suggestions about putting an act together. Davidson is writing a book on the subject, and its outline is blunt. Davidson's reckoning, means opening with an upbeat, well-known number, following it with a medium-tempo current hit, introducing some patter and running through a variety of songs and styles that span the age range of the audience.

Theory is put into practice at the weekly shows campers put on at the nearby Avalon Bowl. For a token $1 admission, tourists get a chance to watch ten student performers do two songs each. Understandably, the performers are something short of polished. On the first weekend, patter ran to lines like "It's really great being here in California" and "Singing is my life." One camper urged the audience to sing along, only to discover none of them knew the words, and another got her heel tangled in the microphone cord. Through it all, David-

son sat out of view of autograph hunters, calmly making notes: "Move a little bit more . . . Don't look down . . . Good sell . . . Great ending."

At the very least, campers end up with tangible results: a 45-minute act that includes songs, patter and jokes and a record of the act. "I've learned how to sell a song," said Jeff Freeman, 21, from Cincinnati. "You don't have to sing beautifully if you can speak a song from your guts." Davidson isn't promising the campers will get work, but most are optimistic. "I expect to have a job somewhere within a week," said Michael Kirkland, 23, from Atlanta. And what of Davidson's plans? For starters, he's going to change the name next summer to "Summer Workshop." "Camp," he has decided, sounds too frivolous.
—Tony Schwartz with Martin Kasindorf

## Star Opens Up A Camp For Singers

SINGER John Davidson has opened a summer camp. But no one will be making wallets or practicing archery — because it's a camp for singers.

One hundred students attend the one-month camp on Catalina Island off the Southern California coast.

"But it's no easy-come, easy-go vacation," said Davidson.

Davidson said he can't guarantee graduates of his camp jobs, but they'll get lots of practical experience.

"They can learn from my experience and from that of other singers like Jack Jones, who will be a guest lecturer. I expect in the crowd there may be a future Sinatra, maybe a John Denver.

"They'll get the chance to make an album and perform live in front of invited audiences of some of the top agents in Hollywood. They'll polish their skills, learn to dance, do a soft shoe routine and lots of gags. They'll also learn about publicity and the business end of showbiz," he said.

"But above all, I want to tell them that you don't have to be a superstar to make it. I never had a hit record. I made it by entertaining people."

Davidson said he had about 20,000 applications for the camp.

H

# Newspaper Clippings

JOHN DAVIDSON'S SINGERS' SUMMER CAMP

CATALINA ISLAND

## Davidson's Summer Camp A Song Workshop For Adults

BY VIRGINIA LUCIER

FRAMINGHAM — "The highs are higher and the lows are lower," but for John Davidson life is more fulfilling at 36 than when he was in his 20s.

Unlike most performers, who dread getting older, the boyish looking entertainer currently performing in the Chateau de Ville Celebrity Series, has no qualms about the aging process. He is enjoying it.

"Everything came so easy when I was younger; now I have to work harder. I'm not competing with another performer, but with my last performance.

"I want to do things now that I never dreamed of then.

On the top of that list is his two-year-old project about to bear fruition and he said "I get so excited just talking about it."

He learned about light opera, German lieder and Broadway while in college, the graduate of Denison University getting B.A. in theatre arts and a minor in music. But he regretted there was no course available on *how to become a popular singer.*

"There was no art form" he recalled. "That's what I want to teach at the John Davidson Singer Summer Camp I'm opening in July.

"There's a private boarding school on Catalina Island and an amphitheatre at the island's tourist center, Avalon, and the two facilities are coming together for this project."

Davidson reported that since his first announcement about the school on the Johnny Carson Show last October, he has received more than 6,000 inquiring letters. His secretary told him, however, it is closer to 8,000 - 9,000.

To date they have received 87 applications from all over the country and these have been accompanied by $100 deposits.

"This will be a non-profit camp,"

he explained. "It will operate four weeks in July and four in August for the purpose of providing an experience of working for anyone 18 or over. We will show the people how they can develop as well-rounded, diversified singing entertainers. In the course of four weeks each person, will record an album of his own.

"Unlike the Doodle Town Pipers, the Young Americans and similar groups, we are creating solo performers.

"The act I presented at the Chateau last night is an example of what I would like to accomplish at the school.

"I've made 12 - 13 albums. I've tried, but I've never had a hit record.

"A hit is a fluke," said Davidson. "Every time you make it, you have to be lucky. John Denver, who hasn't had one in two or three years, has something more in his career.

"You have to have the ability to host a show even if you don't sing; act, as it relates to singing; to move (tap and soft shoe taught me to become more agile); and to know comedy material.

Davidson, who wrote two numbers for his current act, said he will also encourage everyone enrolled in the workshop to write four songs. "You can sit in a classroom and learn, but you have to get up and apply it" he declared.

The singer has cleared his hectic schedule for the first week of each session as he plans to diagram an act for each student. He will also help them with their recording, select material to compose a song to record or to use in an act. A staff of professional people working in show business as a living will be part of the educational camp.

*"It is not necessarily for those who want to play Las Vegas," Davidson explained. I think it will be good also for people involved in arranging entertainment programs for local clubs and luncheon groups."*

The cost per session is $1,600 but the singer feels each person will derive anywhere from $5,000 to $10,000 in educational benefits. "It isn't expensive when you look at it that way" he said. "I think I can save them a lot of time and money."

## Camp For Singers

LOS ANGELES — John Davidson has opened what is believed to be the world's first summer camp for adult pop singers. It's on the island of Santa Catalina, Calif.

The camp, which opened its doors Monday (3), will operate in July and August, with two four-week sessions. It has enrolled 50 students (the maximum the camp will accommodate) for each four-week period.

For the fee, students will receive room and board; have available all music, including a music library arrangements, working with guitar, piano, drums and bass; a record library of numerous live LPs; a book library of biographies of singers; plus private instruction, with each coach taking eight students a day working with each one an hour each day on material.

Students will be afforded an opportunity to perform before a live audience each weekend at the Avalon Bowl, with 10 singers per show.

Each student, upon completion of the course, will have assembled and performed a 45-minute concert and recorded an LP of his or her act. Agents, managers and talent buyers are being invited to look over the available talent.

There will also be instruction in how to approach a label, how to put together a demo tape, selecting the right manager, agent, complementing backup band and how to advance the overall career.

Davidson will have guest speakers for the evening seminars each week. He was the first, to be followed by Kenny Rogers, Jack Jones, Jerry Van Dyke, Ed McMahon and record producers Mike Post and Tom Baylor, and he is talking to others including Leslie Uggams.

"This type of pop singers workshop has never been tried anywhere in the world and we have brought in some of the best instructors including Alexander Hamilton and Tommy Graham. All of these people have put together nightclub acts for singers, worked on record sessions and television specials," says Davidson.

1

## JOHN DAVIDSON'S SINGERS' SUMMER CAMP
## Catalina Island

After a week studying with guest lecturers, setting routines with an arranger, practicing dance movements and studying sight singing, plus the many impromptu sessions with John and the faculty . . .

## ... a live performance at Avalon Bowl.

J

# JDSSC SUMMER PROGRAM FOR 1979
# Enrollment Information

TOTAL FEE (Four Weeks)              $1,600

    SESSION I                    July 8 through August 5
    SESSION II               August 5 through September 2

    There will be 50 students in each session.

JDSSC is a Non-Profit Organization. We are totally supported by your fees, private contributions, ticket and merchandise sales at the Avalon Bowl.

## ADMISSION

We are interested in young professionals, not amateurs, and will accept people on the basis of character and well-rounded personality, as well as musical ability and experience. Students will be chosen by John Davidson and the John Davidson Singers' Summer Camp faculty by reviewing tapes, pictures and resumes. All students must be 18 years of age to apply. The letters of acceptance will be mailed no later than April 1, 1979.

## NOTICE OF NONDISCRIMINATORY POLICY AS TO STUDENTS

The John Davidson Singers' Summer Camp admits students of any race, color, national and ethnic origin to all the rights, privileges, programs and activities generally accorded or made available to students at the Camp. It does not discriminate on the basis of race, color, national and ethnic origin in administration of its educational policies, admissions policies, scholarship and loan programs, and athletic and other Camp-administered programs.

## YOUR APPLICATION SHOULD INCLUDE THE FOLLOWING:

1. List previous singing experience.
2. Knowledge of musical instruments, other than voice, if any.
3. A cassette tape of you singing with simple accompaniment, one ballad and one 'up-tempo' song. **Do not sing with a record.**
4. Full-length picture of yourself.
5. Must have a current health record from your doctor.
6. We will require a $200 registration fee, which will be refundable until April 15, 1979.

    **PLEASE MAKE SURE THAT YOU SEND ALL OF THE ABOVE REQUIREMENTS IN ONE PACKAGE**

## FACULTY

Our faculty will include only working professionals who can share with us their practical experiences and creative ideas. Because of schedules and commitments, we will not actually contract our staff for the Summer of 1979 until late this Spring when they can guarantee their presence. Our staff includes eight (8) vocal coaches, four (4) musicians, a musical director, administrator, sound and stage manager, dance instructor, drama coach and four (4) guest lecturers, rehearsal pianists, lifeguard and a nurse.

# CHAPTER 6

# PERFORMING

*"Whenever I'm on stage, I have a love affair with my audience."*
  —*Judy Garland (quoted in* Weep No More, My Lady *by Mickey Deans)*

**As a singing entertainer,** you never will be able to touch people through television, film, radio or recording the way you can touch them *in person.* The personal appearance is the original form of show business. The tradition of singing in front of gatherings of people, to entertain them, dates back to the days of the very first roving troubadors and wandering minstrels, perhaps even further. It is only in the last 50 years that singing has become something which can be captured and transmitted by mechanical means.

The mechanization of singing began, of course, with the advent of the microphone. While singing with the aid of electronic amplification made a different, more intimate style of vocal delivery possible, it also made the personal appearance by the singer *less* personal. The microphone enabled singers to sing more intimately and be heard better by more people but, at the same time, it created a greater distance—physically and psychologically—between the singer and the audience. We take it for granted today, because we have heard amplified, broadcast and recorded music all our lives, but the very act of passing the human voice through an electronic device had a profound impact on singing as a form of entertainment.

Because of the microphone, first recording, then radio, then talking (and singing) movies and television came along. And singing became a talent which not only could be performed in front of gatherings of people, but also through technological means for audiences unseen by the singer. Recording, radio, film and television made it possible for the singer's voice to be appreciated by listeners who might never see the singer himself or by listeners hundreds or thousands of miles away watching an image on a screen.

Yet, in spite of the fact that electronic technology dominates the modern entertainment business, the fundamental value of performing in person remains unchanged. In spite of television, records, video tape and video discs, performing "live" still is the ultimate challenge for an entertainer. Nothing can replace the excitement, the feeling of sharing and the sense of immediate gratification which exists between performer and audience in a "live" situation.

Furthermore, the best guarantee of success for a singer is the ability to entertain people in person. There is no other medium in which you can work as a performer which provides you with as much artistic (creative) control, money, contact with people and longevity. There's no question that the mass media—television, radio, film and recording—can reach more people and, therefore, make your name a household word. Live performances can't do that. But, unless a performer's success on television or radio, in films or on records is backed up with the ability to captivate audiences in personal appearances, then a media-built career eventually will dry up.

## BASIC RULES OF PERFORMING

Always remember your basic role as a singing entertainer. You are the host(ess) of "a party." When you come out on stage, you should come out as if you are welcoming guests into your home. At home, you wouldn't ignore your guests. You would show them in and make them comfortable. This is exactly what you must do in a live performance. The nightclub, lounge or auditorium is your home, the audience your guests. Reach out and welcome them. Make sure they feel included. Let them get to know you. And when the show is over, thank your guests for coming, just as you would at home. Mentally walk them to the door and say "good-bye" as you would to a friend you might not be seeing for awhile.

These points may seem all too obvious, but many performers fail to project these basic attitudes when entertaining. Never forget that you are the primary catalyst for whatever happens while you're on stage. And never forget that being the catalyst—the master of ceremonies and host(ess)—carries with it certain fundamental responsibilities which you always must meet.

Successful singing entertainers agree that, in everything you say and sing on stage, you must make the audience feel a part of the show and allow them to get to know you. Wayne Newton, for example, made the point in his video taped interview for JDSSC that you must become one of the audience's "friends." "People want to know the performer," he said, "They want to know who you are. You could be teribbly hoarse . . . the band could fall asleep on you . . . but that doesn't matter. The audience is there to get to know *you*. People don't come back to see performers that are not their friends."

In her interview for JDSSC, Lola Falana said she looks at every performance as if it's "my party." Asked what accounts for her remarkable success in personal appearances, she said matter of factly, "Part of it is singing, but it also is touching and being touched, loving and being loved."

Toni Tennille (of the Captain & Tennille) was adamant on the point: "You've got to let people see who you are."

Joe Delaney, a reviewer for the *Las Vegas Sun* who sees some 250 shows in Las Vegas every year, put it this way: "Establish that you're boss . . . and then that you're a *human being*."

Whenever you are on stage, remember these five basic rules of performing:

1. *Own the right to be on stage.* By this we mean you must believe you belong there and show it. Don't go on stage reluctantly with ambivalent feelings. Let the audience know you're certain you want and deserve to be there. Take control of the stage, take charge of the space around you. Be decisive in everything you do.

2. *Respect your elevated position on stage.* Remember, as a performer, you have an elevated position on stage and some people subconsciously resent it. Physically, because of the stage, and psychologically, because you are the center of attention, you are "bigger" and more powerful than the audience. Literally as well as figuratively, they look up to you. With your attitude and humor, get yourself down to the audience's level sometimes. Don't abuse your position.

3. *Remember the importance of eye contact with the audience.* Your eyes are the door between you and your audience. When you close your eyes, you shut the audience out. The audience doesn't feel you care about them or that the song you're singing relates to them. Let the audience *in* by opening your eyes.

4. *Listen to the applause.* Let the audience know that you hear their approval. Remember applause is expected—it's a reflex action, a conditioned response. At the same time, applause is something the audience *needs* to do; it is the lowest common denominator as far as their participation is concerned. When you finish a song, take the microphone away from your mouth, or step away from the mike stand, and let the audience have their moment. Listen. Let it sink in.

5. *Perform for the moment.* Constantly pay attention from one moment to the next to where your show is going. Be aware of the flow, the continuity. Always have a sense of where a particular song is taking you and the audience and how it fits into the overall performance. Be aware of the mood of the audience at all times, and be conscious of the fact that everything you do affects that mood.

## VULNERABILITY

It is appropriate here to mention a very important element in performing live—the *vulnerability* of the performer. Singing entertainers who appear to be flawless and too slick often are respected, but not loved. It's fine to develop your talents to the fullest possible extent and perform with a high degree of professionalism, but if the audience doesn't find some reason to love you and care about you, then you never will be a major star. This chemistry between audience and performer is of critical importance.

Be open. Don't be afraid to let your audience see that you have some of the same feelings and fears they have. Be honest. Study the vulnerability of other singers. Study the vulnerability of children. There is a "little girl" quality or "little boy" quality in most successful entertainers which makes you want to embrace them, even cuddle them as you would a child or a small animal. If the audience senses your need for love, as adults sense a child's need for love, they will want to give you that love. People open their arms to children and small animals because they feel protective of and superior to them. If, as a performer, you come across as invincible, too intellectual or too self-sufficient, the audience will think you don't need them. In this love relationship, they will feel inadequate and, therefore, impotent.

So, let your child-like qualities show on stage. And don't think you don't have them. If you were a totally mature, well-adjusted person, you probably wouldn't feel the need to get up on stage in the first place.


## PACING

Already, we have discussed two of the most effective devices for pacing a show—medleys and audience participation segments. But the pacing of a show involves several other critical factors. We've talked about how each individual song should build to a climax. And we've said a medley should do the same, even though it may involve five or six different songs. The same is true for your entire act—which is simply a bigger collection of songs. Your act must build to a climax or several climaxes.

There are no perfect formulas for pacing a show, no fail-safe methods. But we can give you a blueprint which will enable you to structure your act and, more importantly, understand the dynamics of pacing on stage.

What follows is a suggested program or running order for personal appearances in supper club or nightclub situations. It might not be applicable to every situation, because every performer is unique and every audience is a little different. But it's a starting point for a program that should work in nearly every situation.

## Overture

The overture is the music which is played by your band or by the orchestra before you appear on stage. It should let the audience know something about your musical style. It should be exciting and command the attention of the audience. And, musically, it should say "here is a romantic singing star" or "here comes a sexy lady" or "here comes that good ol' boy." In other words, the overture is your musical signature and it should introduce you to the audience before you appear. If you are following another act, your overture should change the mood. The overture should run approximately 30 seconds.

## Introductory Announcement

Generally in a supper club or nightclub, someone is available to announce you to the audience at the end of the overture. If not, a member of your band can do it. Keep your introduction as simple as possible. There was a time when singers would be introduced with such phrases as "The Midnight Cowboy," "Mr. Music," "A Foxy Lady," "Mr. Entertainment" or "And now, here's the hardest working man in show business . . ." But these are corny and unnecessary. Honesty is the best approach. Don't list a lot of credits. Don't use a lot of adjectives or superlatives. When in doubt, the best introduction is "Ladies and gentlemen . . ." followed by your name.

## Opening Number

The next time you read a news story on the front page of the newspaper, notice how the first three paragraphs of the story set-up the entire story and contain the most important information. The first paragraph, which is called the "lead," should sum up the most important facts. If you read no further, you should know what the story is simply by reading the lead.

On stage, your opening number is your "lead paragraph." An optimistic song, a song that says "I love life," will work. But beware of getting too pushy with songs like "I'm Gonna Live 'Til I Die" or "Curtain Up, Light the Lights." Universal songs about love are good opening numbers. Songs like "I Got the Music In Me" are dangerous because they ignore the audience. Your opening song should be aimed at the audience; it should talk about *them.* There's a selfish reason for doing this—if your attention in the first song is on the audience, their attention will be on you.

"Openers" should be chosen carefully, but keep in mind that during this number, the audience is looking at your outfit, getting used to the way you move, tuning their ears to your vocal sound and, generally, settling down. And, in the same way that you often forget someone's name the first time you're introduced, the audience often will forget your opening number. For this reason, never use special material to open a show. Snappy, special lyrics and intricate rhythms are wasted here. Sing a "public song" to open.

In our video taped interview, Paul Anka made an important observation about another function which is served by your "opener." Anka says that during his "opener" he immediately tries to assess the audience. He asks himself, "What are my problems tonight? How *easy* are they going to be? How *hard* do I have to work?" Anka says if it looks like the audience is not in the palm of his hand, he may sing a ballad later than planned, sing well-known numbers earlier, or attempt to let the audience get to know him sooner by using a "talk spot" or by going into the audience sooner than planned.

## Second Song

You should segue from the first song into the second without talking. There's a reason for this: you want to establish yourself as a singer first. Later, you will establish yourself as a personality. The second spot is a good place for the hottest song of the day. Usually, it will be more relaxed than your opener and allow you an opportunity to settle down. A "shuffle" rhythm which enables you to move around the stage would be good here if you stood center stage for your opener. A relaxed, warm, loose, easy moment works here. If the opener was punchy and stacatto vocally, pick a song for the second spot which lets you sing some long, sustained tones so that by the end of the second song you have established yourself completely as a singer.

Don't let the pace drop. Your first three songs are setting the tone for your entire show. During these songs and your opening talk, you must seduce the audience.

## Opening Talk

The second song should lead into your opening talk. If you are concerned about losing them, and you want to keep the energy up, put a vamp (background musical filler) under this talk which will lead into the third song. Make sure, however, that the band is not so loud that it covers your monologue. This opening talk should be as if you're welcoming people to your home.

## Third Song

A comedy song would work here. If you're a woman, do something to get the women in the audience on your side; if you're a man, do something to get the men on your side. You might do something unexpected, something slightly out of character. If you are sweet and petite, perhaps a raunchy song. If you are "macho," do something cute, perhaps dumb. The effect of the first three songs should be to reveal you both as a singer and a personality.

Good pacing means that you should feel a definite flowing motion in your show, from the minute you come on stage straight through to the end of this third spot. By this time, the audience should be with you. You should have them united as a group. Everyone in the room should feel a part of the show.

Remember the analogy we used earlier: you are the host of a dinner party in your home and the audience is your guest. By the time you have finished your third song, you—as host—should have welcomed your guests, served them an appetizer, soup and salad. Now, you are ready to serve the main course.

## The Heart of Your Show

This segment should consist of songs or a combination of songs and medleys which enable you to give your best performances as a singer and interpreter of music. This is the heart of your performance, the segment which is most important to you. You may do a medley; you may sit on a stool and sing a ballad; you may sing an unfamiliar song or a song you've written. The point is, you can indulge yourself a little in this segment. Sing what you want to sing so long as it speaks, in some way, to the audience. This is your chance to touch them with your music.

In the heart of your show, you can be as artful as you want. By this time, you have won the right. You don't have to be funny; you can be sensitive, vulnerable, thoughtful or provocative. Naturally, the more well-known your material is, the better it will score. But don't be afraid to take some chances at this point. This is your moment.

The conclusion of this segment should get extended applause and give you an opportunity to take your first bow. You even may be able to walk off stage while the band plays your "bow music." In any case, when you conclude the heart of your show, let the audience know that you think you have just done your best.

## "The Clincher"

If the overture, the first three songs and the opening talk are the equivalent of an appetizer, soup and salad, and if the heart of your show is the equivalent of the main course, then the "clincher"—the final segment before your closing number—is desert and coffee.

The heart of your show is for you. But the "clincher" is for the audience. It is the time when you should indulge their wishes and tastes and, in a sense, reward them for allowing you to indulge yourself in the previous segment. It is the time when you can do an audience participation segment most effectively.

We have discussed ideas for audience participation. If you have a musical segment which involves the audience, gets them going, this is the time to do it. You may take requests, bring someone on stage, stroll through the audience and sing songs intimately to them or lead the audience in a sing-a-long. Find a premise which will enable you to have fun with music and people, something up-beat, warm, friendly and endearing.

The "clincher" segment should lead you into your closing number.

## Closing Number

There are many ways to close a show. If you are performing for an older group, it may be best to close with a thoughtful, up-lifting moment. If they are younger, you may want to leave them with high energy and excitement. Either approach will work. If you have done a thoughtful number in the heart of your show, then probably you should balance your act at this point with an exciting number. On the other hand, if the thing you do best in the heart of your act involves high energy and hard-driving rhythms, then you may want to close with something more subtle, something elegant with a universal message. If you use a thoughtful or provocative closing number, be sure you don't start preaching. It's not your job to change the way people think.

You'll be far more effective if you share a great thought or moment and let the audience make its own judgment.

## Variety and Balance

Keep in mind throughout your act that *variety* and *balance* are essential to holding the audience's interest. Never allow your show to become too heavily weighted in any one direction. When you are assembling the musical segments in your act, try to incorporate a variety of songs—up-beat numbers, love ballads, dramatic songs, country songs, rock and roll songs, comedy songs, up-lifting songs, Top 40 songs and old fashioned songs.

Variety also is important in the way songs end, in the way you move on stage and in the way you talk to the audience. For example, while every song should build to a climax and have a strong ending, all the endings shouldn't sound the same. If you have a favorite dance step which you like to use during rock, disco or other high energy numbers, don't repeat the same movements every time. It becomes monotonous. When you find a good phrase to introduce a particular song, use it for that song but don't keep using it again and again.

Your show never will build if you simply string songs together like so many pieces of laundry on a clothesline. A graph of your show should not appear as a straight, horizontal line. Rather, a graph of a well-paced and well-balanced show should appear as a line which starts high, levels off, perhaps dips down for a segment, then ascends again to a new high point by your closing number. Your show should be dynamic, not static. It should have peaks, valleys (though never too deep), plateaus and end on a peak.

Remember that pacing on stage is extremely important. As Paul Anka so aptly put it, "You've got to stroke, you've got to touch, and you've got to build." (See graph of "Pacing Your Show.")

DIAGRAM OF PACING A COMPLETE SHOW AND GRAPH OF INTENSITY

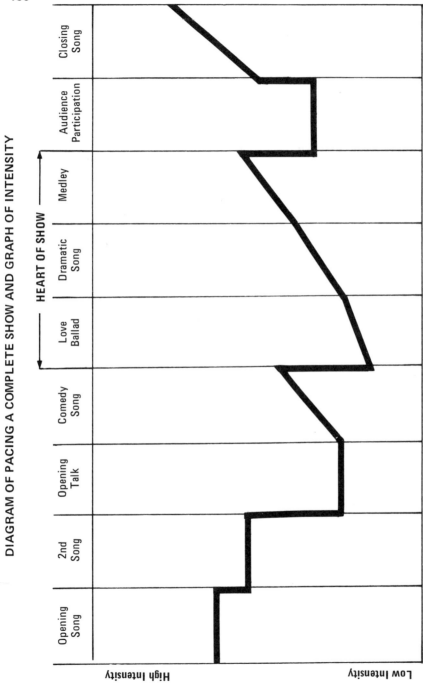

## MUSICAL TRICKS

There are a number of musical tricks which help in pacing a show. First, there is the *vamp*. A vamp is where the band plays a certain section of a song continuously until you are ready to start singing. You always should have a vamp at the beginning of your opening song. This allows you time to make your entrance and wait until the applause has subsided before you start the song. The band vamps and, when you're ready, you sing. It also is possible to use a vamp *during* a song, in which case the band plays a certain section of the song continuously until you are ready to resume singing. A vamp can be used effectively to keep the pace of the show going while you are talking to the audience or doing some piece of business. The band should vamp, for example, while you mop the sweat from your brow, take a drink of water or, if you're like Elvis, throw scarves into the audience.

Another tool for pacing is *transitional music.* Transitional music, as the term implies, is a short piece of music written specifically to cover any sort of technical transition in the show. If you leave the stage to change your wardrobe, the band should play transitional music. Transitional music also fills what otherwise would be a void when you have set changes, when you are setting a microphone, a stool or other props, or when you are bringing someone to the stage.

*Tags* or tag endings are a musical trick designed to increase audience response. A tag is a short musical refrain, usually eight bars long, which the band plays immediately after a song ends, while the audience is applauding. The singer doesn't sing on the tag. The tag merely restates the final melodic phrase of the song for emphasis. Wayne Newton is a master of the tag ending as a means to maximize audience response to the song he has just sung.

The last piece of music you hear in a show should be the *bows.* The bows are a musical trick which allow you to leave the stage while the band is still playing. And, usually, while the band plays the bows, the audience, expecting you to return to take a bow, will continue to applaud. If the band stops playing after the last song and doesn't play bows, you'll have no play-off—no music to cover your exit and your

DIAGRAM OF PACING A COMPLETE SHOW WITH MUSICAL TRICKS AND GRAPH OF INTENSITY

HEART OF SHOW

Vamp | Opening Song | 2nd Song | Opening Talk over vamp | Comedy Song | Love Ballad | Dramatic Song | Medley | Tag of last song in medley | Audience Participation | Transitional Music | Hit song as closing number | Bows based on hit record

High Intensity

Low Intensity

return. Bow music should be either majestic and important or exciting and hard-driving. It shouldn't just be nice. It must be a piece of music which demands a response. In some cases, a singer who is known for a particular song may use a refrain from that song both in the overture and in the bows. To be effective, though, the melody must be given either a majestic or an exciting, hard-driving interpretation.

There's one more trick—the placement of your hit record(s), if you are lucky enough to have one (or more). Put your biggest hit in the show where it will have the maximum effect, either in the opening or the closing. Using your hit as an opener will give you instant identity. Using your hit as a closer will give you instant excitement. (See graph of "Pacing" with addition of musical tricks.)

## MANAGING THE AUDIENCE

A fundamental aspect of the art of the singing entertainer is managing or manipulating an audience. With what you sing, with pacing, with musical tricks, you can control, to a large extent, how an audience reacts. This is why singing entertainment truly is an art form. The art lies in the fact the audience seldom realizes it is being manipulated. Be aware of this. Also, keep these two things in mind: (1) You must lead the audience through your show from moment to moment; and (2) You must *not* demand the same level of attention from the audience all of the time.

With respect to the first point, always remember you are the only one who knows what your show is designed to do and where it is designed to go. Without revealing your techniques—your devices and tricks—you must be the one who lets the audience know (a) that you have a plan for their enjoyment, a map for the journey you're taking them on; and (b) what that plan is as your journey progresses.

In terms of the second point—managing the audience's attention— you must understand that, like you, the audience cannot maintain the same level of intensity all of the time. From time to time, you must let them off the hook, allow them to recharge their enthusiasm. If you insist on the same level of attention and response at all times, you will exhaust the audience and lose them.


## BODY AND MIND ON STAGE

Performing, except on radio or on records, is a visual medium. Thus, on stage your body is an instrument you must play for visual effect. To be an exciting, vital performer, it's not enough simply to stand or sit in one place for an entire performance. Your body movement should help communicate, in a natural way, what you're singing. If you're singing a disco song and you don't move, that would be *unnatural.* If you're singing a love ballad and you move around too much, it will be distracting. For dramatic moments, stand still or, perhaps, take a few deliberate steps. During your opening number, appear alive and animated. Be aware that even when you're not dancing or moving around the stage deliberately, your *body language*—posture, stance, the position of your shoulders, arms and hands—says as much as to the audience as what you are singing. On stage, your body is an extension of your mind.

Avoid using phony gestures or overly-dramatic gestures unless, of course, they are for comedic effect. Avoid especially the "limp wrist syndrome." This is where the singer allows one hand to hang limply from the wrist. You may think this looks nonchalant, but it is a useless affectation which can be very distracting.

Your gestures should mean something and appear to be a natural part of whatever you are trying to express. Never supply motion unless you *feel* it. The way you move on stage should flow with the music and never break that flow. In the same way that you want to sing in tune, you must appear to be in tune physically.

When you end a song, let your body movement tell the audience that the song has ended. Here you can afford to be a little more dramatic. It's okay to thrust one arm in the air to catch the final downbeat of the ending. Look at it as though you are providing punctuation—a period, an exclamation mark—at the end of a phrase.

# BODY POSITION

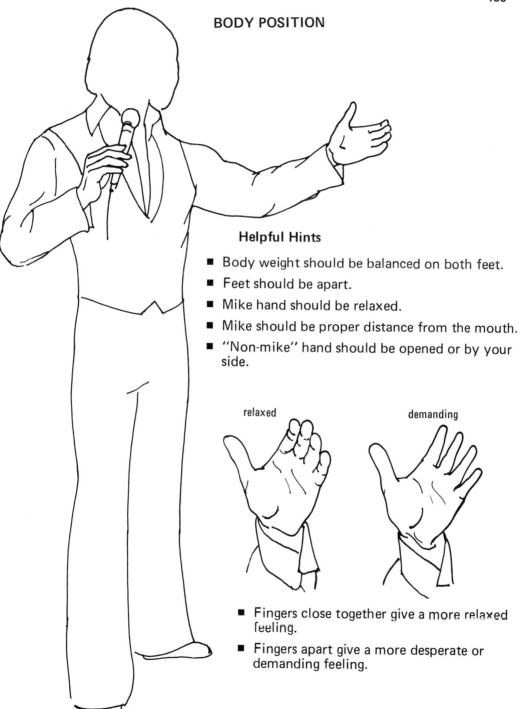

## Helpful Hints

- Body weight should be balanced on both feet.
- Feet should be apart.
- Mike hand should be relaxed.
- Mike should be proper distance from the mouth.
- "Non-mike" hand should be opened or by your side.

relaxed          demanding

- Fingers close together give a more relaxed feeling.
- Fingers apart give a more desperate or demanding feeling.

# BODY POSITION (Cont'd.)

## Feet Positions Facing Forward

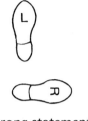

Strong statement
"assertive"

Strong statement
"positive"

Weak statement
"sweet"

Weak statement
"insecure"

Standing sideways but looking forward. Conveys intimacy and makes body line appealing.

**Limp Wrist**

Overly casual, seldom effective. Implies singer thinks he's "cool". This gesture is to blazé. By turning hand over, palm up, an open feeling is projected and useful gestures can follow.

Traveling back and forth across the stage as well as up and down stage, is an effective way to take command of the stage area. And, depending on where you move and when, these movements can lend emphasis to what you're singing. In your mind, divide the stage into four equal sections. Imagine there is a line running from stage left to stage right which cuts the stage in half; imaging there is another line in the center of the stage running from the front edge where the audience is (down-stage) back towards the orchestra (up-stage). (See graph pg. 138.)

When you first come on stage for your "opener", or anytime you're singing an up-tempo number where you want to communicate physical energy, use the two front or down-stage areas (A & B). If you are trying to create a dramatic moment, begin center stage in the rear or up-stage sections (C & D) further away from the audience. Then, for emphasis and greater dramatic impact, move deliberately forward (down-stage) toward the end of the song.

As a general rule, sing the verses of a song in the front or down-stage half of the stage. The reason for this is the verses in a song typically are more personal, more conversational and, therefore, are more effective if delivered intimately down stage. For the choruses, which typically are less intimate lyrically and larger musically, you can afford to move up stage away from the audience.

We talked earlier about eye contact. Now a few words about facial expressions. The more relaxed you appear on stage, the more natural in every sense, the more appealing you will be as a performer. If you are straining vocally or if you are worried or scared, the first place it shows is in your face. Be aware of this fact, and try to project confidence, warmth and sincerity with facial expressions. But never resort to artificial expressions. When you are speaking, your facial expressions change naturally. The same should be true when you're singing. Don't contort your face to try to make people believe you're feeling the song, just feel the song. On the other hand, don't allow your face to become a frozen, lifeless mask. Though no one likes to watch a singer who constantly has a smile plastered across his face, smiling on stage when you're singing (unless a smile would spoil the intimacy or dramatic effect) generally is a good idea. Perhaps the best advice is: forget about

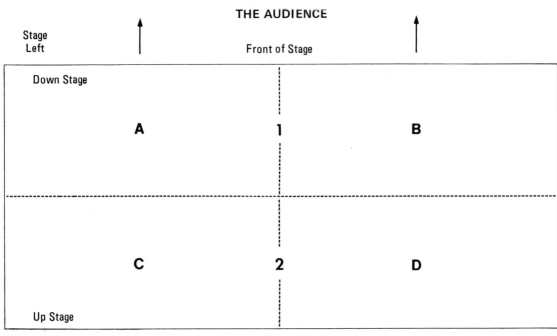

SECTION 1 — Sing the VERSES of a song on the front half of the stage closest to the audience.

SECTION 2 — Move back for the CHORUSES toward the band or orchestra.

SECTIONS A & B — Use the front portion of the stage for your opening song and other up-beat songs.

SECTIONS B & C — Use the rear portion of the stage for dramatic moments where you wish to be stationary, then move forward into Sections A & B if you wish to increase the dramatic effect.

your face. Concentrate on what you are singing, and let your face naturally reflect your feelings.

## MICROPHONE TECHNIQUE

Never play with the mike cord. There is nothing more distracting. Concentrate on using the mike to your best advantage. Forget about the cord.

Keep the mike out of your face as much as possible. If you're singing into a mike on a stand, be sure the mike isn't so high that it blocks your face. Position the mike so that it's pointing at your chin, just below your mouth. Then stand back two or three inches. The mike now will be in a good position to pick up your voice, yet not obscure you. When using a mike without a stand (a hand mike), observe the same basic rule. Hold the mike at or slightly below your chin and sing over the top of it. Your voice will be heard and your face will be seen. Microphones are sensitive, so remember you don't have to "eat" or "swallow" the mike for it to operate effectively. In fact, most microphones operate more efficiently when kept a few inches away from the source of the sound to be amplified.

Hold the microphone in one hand. Balance it comfortably so that you can hang on to it securely, but don't hold it in a vice grip. Generally, it is best to hold the mike between your fingers and your thumb. This is particularly true for women. When a woman holds a mike the way she'd hold an ice cream cone or grip a ski pole, it appears less feminine, less refined. However, gripping the microphone more firmly may be necessary at times or may be done for comedic, dramatic or sensual effect.

Alright, you have the mike in one hand, say your right hand. You're holding it between your fingers and your thumb. Your elbow is bent slightly. Bring your elbow in towards your waist until the elbow and the upper part of your arm are next to your body. Move your forearm up or down so that the microphone is in the proper position at or slightly beneath your chin. Now, *lock your elbow.* Keeping your elbow

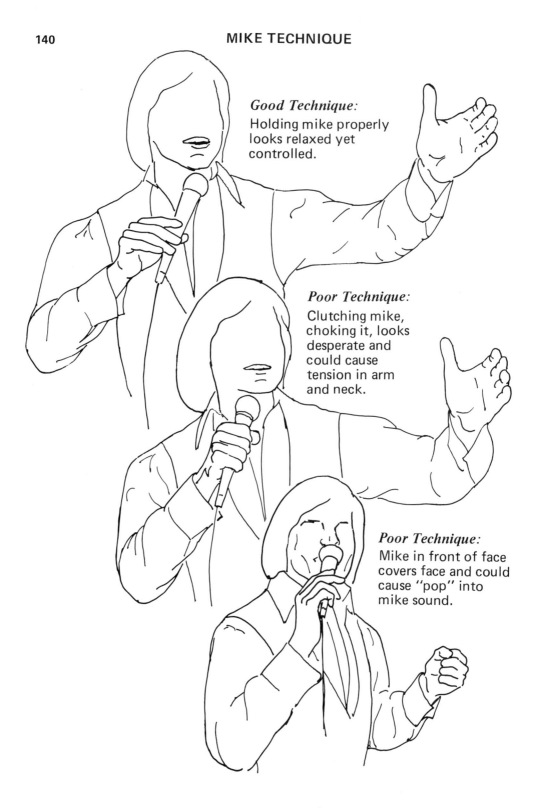

*Good Technique:*
Holding mike properly
looks relaxed yet
controlled.

*Poor Technique:*
Clutching mike,
choking it, looks
desperate and
could cause
tension in arm
and neck.

*Poor Technique:*
Mike in front of face
covers face and could
cause "pop" into
mike sound.

locked and at your side, notice that no matter how the rest of your body moves, the microphone remains in the proper place for singing. The mike becomes an extension of your body and the audience now will forget about it and pay more attention to your singing.

When you finish a song, take the mike down from your face—drop your forearm to your side—and let the audience know the song is over.

Also, notice how the microphone affects the presence and the high and low tones in your voice. If you hold the mike too far from your mouth when you're speaking, your voice will be heard, but it will have no real presence. If you speak right on the mike, your voice will have much greater presence and, therefore, greater authority. Did you ever notice how the host of "The Tonight Show" uses his *desk* microphone for emphasis? Guests on the show are miked with what is called a "boom," an omni-directional mike held over their heads out of view of the camera. The host's voice, on the other hand, primarily is picked up by that mike sitting on the desk in front of him. And when he wants to be sure the audience hears one of his ad lib remarks, he leans in and, without raising his voice, delivers it right on the mike. The presence insures the impact. By speaking softly on the mike, you can communicate very intimately with your audience. Your distance from the mike also affects the *tone* of your voice. Notice that when you're close to the mike, it accentuates your *lows*. Backing away from the mike accentuates your *highs*.

## TYPES OF AUDIENCES

Some performers change their show for different parts of the country and different audiences. They argue that one type of show won't work in every situation. Other performers insist that the right show with the right material can be played anywhere, to any audience. Should you change your nightclub act when you do concerts? Should you eliminate certain material that works in Las Vegas for fear that it won't work in Des Moines or Denver?

If you have put together a successful act which consistently gets the response you think it deserves, probably there is no reason to change the pacing of the act. It is true that in concert the audience is seated more formally in rows of chairs and, therefore, is prepared to be more attentive. In nightclubs, you have more informal seating and, of course, people are eating, drinking and moving around. But once you develop a certain type of performance routine which involves a certain balance of up-tempo songs, ballads, comedy segments, medleys and audience participation, you should use this format in every performance. Indeed, as you become known, your audiences will expect it of you.

It used to be that different parts of the country were more liberal than others. This is changing. Nowadays, although there are pockets of conservatism, and certainly Los Angeles and New York audiences still are more progressive than most others, audiences everywhere are more sophisticated. This is largely due to the effect which television and movies have had in recent years. Now, wherever you live in the country, you know what's going on in the rest of the country. So, your best material should be effective from coast to coast, nevertheless, let's examine the outstanding characteristics of different types of audiences.

If you're singing for a group of older people, people say in their 50's and 60's or older, you may notice that their response is subdued. Generally, older people appreciate you more than they show. It makes sense, when you think about it. Older audiences are less excitable and less inclined to be demonstrative. The opposite often is true of teenagers and children. Younger people are more excitable and, as an audience, usually more eager to please. Generally, teenagers and children show more appreciation than they really feel. With youth comes exhuberance. Young audiences are more anxious and more willing to be demonstrative.

College audiences, as a rule, are the sharpest and most sophisticated. Although they are more reserved than teenagers and children, they tend to be enthusiastic and expressive. You should realize, however, that college groups also are opinionated and influenced by current trends. They are the most contemporary. They support current fashions, currently popular entertainers and current trends in music, television and motion pictures. When you perform for college students, you must reflect their contemporary attitudes and interests.

Las Vegas audiences represent the best cross-section of America. Granted, they are not the most contemporary, but neither are they unsophisticated. They are average. Be aware, however, that a Las Vegas audience almost always is exhausted and over-stimulated. The pace of life for visitors in Las Vegas is hectic and the hours are late. Also, shows in Las Vegas are expensive. In 1979, the cost of seeing a dinner show, including gratuities, was as high as $60 to $75 for two people. When people are paying this much money to see you, and they are tired and dazed by the glitter of The Strip, they become demanding and difficult to impress. In Las Vegas, an ordinary show isn't enough. It must be special. Everytime you go on stage you must "wow" them. Your show must have excitement, production values (for example, dancers, singers, video screens, elaborate sets and so on), and you must always go that extra distance as an entertainer.

Audiences at state fairs around the country probably are the most uninhibited. Of course, the physical set-up for a performance at a state fair, usually out doors in an amphitheater, football stadium or exhibition area, makes it difficult to hold the crowd's attention. There are distractions such as people coming and going, the summer heat and vendors working in the audience. But, typically, a state fair audience is ready to have a good time. If the accent in your show is on fun and the feeling is up-beat, fair audiences can be more demonstrative than any other.

Television studio audiences frequently are in awe of the studio itself. They are fascinated with the cameras, the lights, the sets, the cast and crew. They also are instructed and conditioned to respond and realize very quickly that they are part of the show. They applaud when the "applause" sign goes on. They wait patiently when there are technical difficulties or other delays. Also, a television studio audience is conditioned to expect a certain quality of entertainment. The mere fact that a performer is appearing on television gives him or her instant credibility. The audience assumes you must be reasonably good, or you wouldn't be on the show. The most important thing to remember when you're performing on television, though, is to *play to the cameras.* There may be only 300 or 400 people in the studio, but there may be ten or twenty million viewers at home. Those people at home are your audience. Play to them.

Private parties and conventions can be among the most difficult because they feel free to make demands on you that others would not make. When you play for a private party or convention, you are expected to become a part of the party or the convention. But, as a rule, these audiences are less inhibited because everyone knows everyone else. The familiarity makes them more demonstrative. Also, when you know that your audience has one thing in common, i.e., they all work for Century 21 Real Estate or the Ford Motor Company, then they are easier to approach. If you incorporate a few jokes or a segment in your act to capitalize on the fact that everyone present has one think in common or, in other words, you play to their special interests as a group, you will be enthusiastically received.

## INTENSITY VS. INTENT

What, if anything, should you change about your performance when working in different media—small rooms, amphitheaters, television and recording?

We have said that, in most cases, you will not have to alter the pacing of your show, the basic structure of your act. We have said that you don't have to change the material in your act, except in certain circumstances where you wish to incorporate material which will appeal to the special interests of an audience or its locale. The one thing which you must change, however, depending on the medium in which you are working, is the *intensity* of your performance. That is, the size, the "hotness" of your performance should change according to the medium.

You may have heard the expression, "He wasn't right for the room," applied to entertainers. What this means is that the performer, for one reason or another, failed to adapt to the medium or the performing situation. In some instances, of course, this may mean the performer's material wasn't right for the audience. But let's assume, for the sake of discussion, that material is a constant, that is, you already have an act which has proven its worthiness in a variety of situations. It has universal appeal. How, then, could you be wrong for the room? The answer lies not in the material but in the intensity of the performance.

Marshall McLuhan wrote a book several years ago called, *The Medium Is the Message.* If you haven't read it, do so. In the book, McLuhan suggests why certain performers are successful on television and other equally talented performers are not. His premise, very simply, is that, because it is an electronic medium, television is a "cool" medium, and the performers who are most successful on TV are "cool performers." If a performer is too "hot"—his or her performance or personality is too intense, too big—that performer will not come across successfully on TV.

What makes TV a "cool medium?"

First, it is an electronic medium which comes into your home. Hence, it is intimate, in that sense. Second, the TV screen is small (by comparison to motion picture screens), it has rather poor resolution (clarity of image) and, therefore, does not demand your undivided attention as would a singer on stage or an actor on the screen. Finally, TV is a highly accessible medium. Most people have televisions; the average TV set is on for something like six hours a day; and TV has become the predominant centerpiece in most homes. As TV producer-executive Bob Shanks has observed in his book, *The Cool Fire,* the television set has replaced the fireplace in the American living room.

Undoubtedly you have seen examples of McLuhan's premise on TV. The most successful singers on television have been such "cool personalities" as Bing Crosby, Perry Como, Andy Williams and Dean Martin. Hard-sell or "hot" personalities or performers who are accustomed to performing "big" typically are not as successful on television. This is why singers like Sammy Davis, Jr., Ben Vereen and Wayne Newton strive to tone down on television the intensity which they use so effectively in live situations.

The intensity of performance needed in each different performing medium—from singing to one person to singing on records or TV to singing on the Broadway stage—can be seen on a graph (see Intensity of Performance graph, p. 147).

The performance which requires the least intensity would be a one-on-one performance. If you are singing to one person in your living room, you need very little intensity in your performance to reach your listener. A comparatively small, "cool" performance in such an intimate situation will enable you to create the desired effect. Likewise, if you over-perform for an audience of one—if you're too intense, too "hot"— you will spoil the intimacy of the situation and lose your listener.

But the intensity of a performance must suit the medium in which you're performing. Let's say you go into the studio to make a record. You may wish to use the same intensity you used performing intimately, one-on-one. Or you may have to make your performance a little bigger, a little "hotter," Still, recording—again, primarily because it is electronic—is a relatively "cool" medium. Like TV, you don't want to over-power the microphone by making your perforance too intense. Hence, as on TV, you must find a level of intensity for your performance which is consistent with the medium.

Moving up the intensity scale, notice how the intensity of performance used on television falls within the range of intensity used in recording. Both recording and TV are comparatively "cool" media. But if you're recording a ballad, your intensity will be (or should be) somewhat less than if you're recording a high energy rock song. Your vocal performance on a song like "It's Impossible" would be less intense than on a song like "Johnny B. Goode."

The size of the room in which you're performing also dictates the size of your performance. In a small, intimate room, if your performance is too big, you will overpower your audience. Your intensity won't be right for the medium (the room). However, if you're playing to 3,000 seats or, as many acts do, to 15,000 or 20,000 seats, you must increase the size of your performance. You must be bigger, more expansive and more demonstrative. This applies not only to your vocal performance, but also to your gestures, timing and movements.

SIZE OR "HOTNESS' OR INTENSITY OF PERFORMANCE

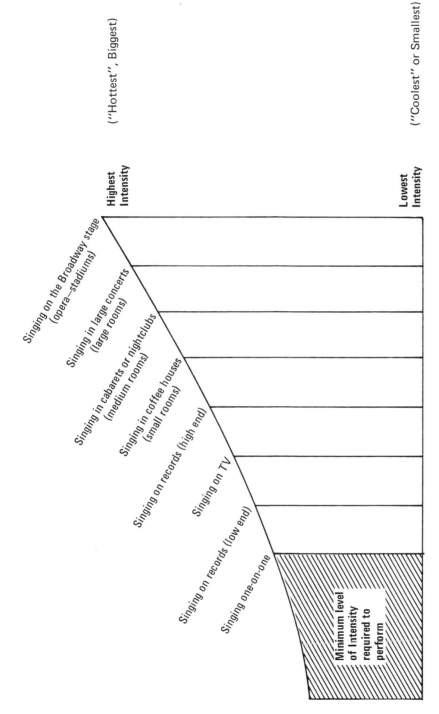

("Hottest", Biggest)

Highest Intensity

Singing on the Broadway stage (opera—stadiums)

Singing in large concerts (large rooms)

Singing in cabarets or nightclubs (medium rooms)

Singing in coffee houses (small rooms)

Singing on records (high end)

Singing on TV

Singing on records (low end)

Singing one-on-one

Minimum level of Intensity required to perform

Lowest Intensity

("Coolest" or Smallest)

At the high end of the intensity scale is Broadway, opera and legitimate theater. On the Broadway stage, the singer's intensity must be great enough to reach the back of the theater. Usually, he does not have the benefit of using a hand-held mike, but rather must rely on voice projection. This also is true for opera singers. You may have noticed how rarely an opera singer comes across well on television. The reason now should be evident. The opera singer is accustomed to having to give a big performance on stage. And the intensity of the opera singer's performance typically is *not* compatible with the intensity of performance most effective in the medium of television.

As you study the graph and think about this, keep in mind the difference between intensity and *intent.* Intent is the purpose, or motivation behind what you do. It is an internal thing. Intensity is the size (bigness or smallness), volume (loudness or softness), and temperature ("hotness" or "coolness") of what you do. Notice that when you *decrease* your intensity, it may be necessary or effective to *increase* your intent. This is what an actor like Marlon Brando does when he wants a softly spoken line to have the impact of a command or a scream. Also, if your intent is clear, you can get away with using less intensity and still communicate a thought effectively.

## EVALUATING PERFORMANCES

Let's say you've just come off stage and feel your show was "off." You're sitting there with your musicians, and you want to know what went wrong. Consider these often overlooked possibilities:

If you felt the tempos were too fast, it could mean that in this particular performance, you were so involved in the lyrics that it threw off your timing in making the transitions between phrases. Perhaps when you routined the song, you weren't thinking so much about the lyrics or they didn't mean as much to you, so a brighter tempo felt good. Of course, there is a possibility the musicians were rushing the tempo during the performance. But if all the musicians say the tempos were normal, then you must realize that your intent may have increased during the song. That is, songs felt rushed, because you were making more of a commitment to the material than in previous performances and you needed more time to dwell on the lyrics.

If you come off stage and complain that all the tempos were too slow, but all the musicians assure you that the tempos were the same as the night before, then probably you were not as focused—your intent was not as strong as on previous nights. When your mind wanders and you're not thinking about what you are singing, you'll feel like every song is dragging.

Tempos also may seem slow and you may find yourself increasing your *intensity* if you become distracted by wanting to impress someone in particular in the audience. This is a natural tendency. However, if you notice yourself doing this, try instead to increase your *intent.* Forget whomever you may be trying to impress. Concentrate on someone in the audience you don't know.

If you felt your voice was not loud enough in the monitors, there could be several reasons for this. There is, of course, always the possibility that something is wrong with the sound equipment. But the reason may lie in the fact that you didn't have the edge (the "bite") in your voice which made your voice appear to have more volume last night. Or perhaps you weren't breathing or controlling the flow of air correctly to produce a louder sound. If you're sure it wasn't you, then see if perhaps the band's volume was louder and was drowning you out.

Always hold this thought: the biggest variables on stage during any performance are you and your voice. So, before you accuse or fire anybody after a show, settle down and ask yourself, "Was it me?"

## WHAT TO DO IF THE SHOW ISN'T WORKING

What should you do if, in the middle of a show, you feel nothing is working? Some performers will charge the show run-down (ordering of songs) while on stage in an attempt rescue the performance. Rarely is this a good idea. If your run-down is wrong, it's wrong. Change it later.

But don't panic while you're on stage. Try to continue to give the best performance you can give. Consistency is very important. Keep your perspective. Perhaps the audience is slow. Perhaps you still can reach them. Re-double your effort. Never give up. If you appear to be having a good time, and if you can get a few other people with you, still more people will follow.

Personal appearances are the ultimate challenge for a singing entertainer. Unlike recording or television where you may have a second chance, in live performances you have only one chance to affect the audience. In the fleeting time which it takes to do a show, your art is created, judged and discarded. Once you leave the stage, your creation is gone. Performing live is art for the moment. So, make every moment count.

CHAPTER 7

# VOCAL STAMINA AND FATIGUE

*"My voice alone is just an ordinary voice. What people come to see is how I use it."*

*—Elvis Presley (Quoted in* The Great American Popular Singers *by Henry Pleasants)*

**Of all the various types of singers,** including those who sing opera, light opera, Broadway musicals or religious music, no one demands more of his vocal mechanism than the contemporary pop singer.

Opera singers sing a maximum of three performances a week, and the vocally taxing moments in any given performance usually are followed by periods of rest. After singing an aria, for example, the opera singer frequently is able to leave the stage to prepare for the next entrance.

Broadway singers perform eight shows a week but, within a musical that lasts an hour and 45 minutes, an individual sings for no more than a half an hour. The rest of the time the performer is delivering dialogue, and there are moments when the singer gets to rest off-stage.

Singers of religious music generally perform only one day a week and, even if they perform more often, usually they sing no more than one or two selections during a performance.

Pop singers, on the other hand, frequently arc asked to do 18 or more performances a week, in which they sing for an hour or more in a smoke-filled room with very little time to rest between numbers.

Pop music is extremely demanding vocally for several other reasons. In most other styles of music, the accompaniment and arrangements are designed to favor the singer. But in pop music, the singer often has to compete with the band and sometimes has to produce a vocal tone which he can't even hear. What's more, because of the microphone and amplification, the pop singer is more detached from his vocal sound. Consequently, it is more difficult for the pop singer to judge how well he is using the vocal mechanism. In this respect, opera, Broadway and classical singers have a distinct advantage. They can hear their voice in its natural state and, therefore, are better able to evaluate how they are singing. Finally, no other singer is expected to do so many other things while singing. The pop singer must sing as artfully as possible while constantly varying his performance to entertain fully. The popular singing entertainer is concerned not only with moving the vocal chords, but also with moving the listener by what he does and says on stage which, in addition to singing, may include dancing, performing comedy or moving through the audience.

Hence, if you want to sing pop music for a living, it is essential to develop tremendous vocal stamina and avoid vocal fatigue. Stamina, of course, comes with time. Your vocal chords are muscles. The more you use them correctly, the stronger they get. But, like any muscle, the vocal chords can become strained or fatigued. They have their limits, and you must take care of them.

## WARMING UP

What follows are some tips which have been suggested by various contemporary singing entertainers.

One of the best ways to avoid vocal fatigue is to find a way to warm up—vocally, physically and mentally—before each performance. If your first show is at eight o'clock at night, the time to start warming up your voice is the minute you get up in the morning. Start by getting your "head voice" going; hum the falsetto tones which cause your vocal chords to stretch and "thin out," giving you a light, airy sound.

Remember that your speaking voice, which you use most of the time, is a "chest voice." The higher tones, "head tones," must be encouraged to ring all day long, even while you're speaking.

By four or five o'clock in the afternoon, you should attempt some light vocalizing to further limber up your vocal chords. Use a pitch pipe, piano, guitar or tuning fork to get a note, then begin to exercise. If you're stuck in a motel room or some other place where an instrument or pitch pipe isn't available, pick up the telephone. In most cases, the dial tone is a B-flat or an F. Find out what note the dial tone is in your area and you'll always be able to pick up the phone and get that note. Regardless of what note the tone is, you will have a starting point for your exercises. It is important to exercise with some sense of relative pitch in mind so that you don't needlessly strain your voice while you determine the range in which your voice is strongest on a particular day. If your voice seems more resonant or stronger in a higher or lower range than the day before, don't be alarmed. This is natural. Your voice changes depending on how you've used it, the humidity, the quality of the air, the temperature and any number of other factors.

Physical exercise during the day which makes you pant and breathe deeply and gets the blood flowing through your body will make you sing better at night. Remember that you sing with air and muscle. The more control you have over each, the better you'll be able to sing.

Avoid talking excessively during the day, especially on the telephone. Talking is more tiring than singing because, when we talk, we seldom remember to support the vocal mechanism with a column of air from the diaphragm.

Also, remember that being with people is a strain, both physically and emotionally. If you're performing at night, be sure to spend some time alone during the day. Most experts agree that singing is more mental than physical. Stress or frustration in your personal life will show up in your voice. Before each performance, set aside at least 15 minutes to warm up mentally. Experiment with meditation, yoga and other methods of relaxation and focusing your energy. Obviously, what works for one performer might not work for another. But if you find a device that enables you to compose yourself before the show, incorporate it into your daily warm-up routine.

A half hour before a performance, drink only hot liquids. Your vocal chords are located in the larynx just above the trachea (wind pipe) and are, in a sense, the "door" to your lungs. When you swallow, this "door" closes involuntarily to prevent anything from going into the lungs. So, what you drink doesn't actually come into contact with the vocal chords themselves. However, hot tea, coffee, Sanka, hot water with lemon and/or honey or any hot beverage warms your throat and, by the process of heat transference, warms your vocal chords. Hot liquids also encourage blood flow, while cold liquids restrict blood flow. Just as a dancer doesn't attempt to dance when his muscles are cold, neither should you attempt to exercise your vocal chords until they are warm and limber.

The only way to lubricate your vocal chords directly (topically) is by inhaling some sort of moisture—steam from a tea kettle, sink or steam room or mist from an atomizer. If you are working in a dry climate such as Las Vegas, taking some steam every day is a good way to prevent the vocal chords from becoming excessively dry and brittle. This drying of the chords is what is commonly referred to as "Las Vegas throat."

Some singers feel that certain foods, such as dairy products, create excess mucous and should, therefore, be avoided just before singing. Avoidance of such foods is an individual matter. If you have phlegm on your vocal chords, chances are that it is drainage which has fallen either from your sinuses or from the nasal passages. When clearing this phlegm away, in other words when clearing your throat, do so very gently by forcing lots of air over the chords. Clearing your throat harshly jars the vocal chords and is unnecessarily hard on them.

The survey of singers conducted for this book indicates the way in which successful singers warm up for a performance varies greatly. 25% of those who responded said they warm-up by doing some form of mental exercise only. 25% said they use *one* of the three methods for warming up, and 25% said they warm up by doing all three types of exercises—vocal, physical and mental and 25% said they do nothing to warm up at all.

Most singers agree, however, that too much talking and interaction with people before a performance does affect your voice. Johnny Mathis, in an interview in the *Los Angeles Times* (October 29, 1978), put it this way: "People are nice, they want to talk and visit with a touring singer, but Mother Nature just didn't build my voice to do lots of sociable visiting before or after I do a concert. I stay close to my room and lead a quiet life."

## SCHEDULING REHEARSALS AND SHOWS

Singers frequently complain about having to sing in the morning or early in the day. If they have not warmed up adequately, they make excuses: "It's too early to sing" or "My voice isn't awake yet." The fact is, no matter what time a rehearsal or show is, you should be ready to sing. Of course, earlier in the day, your voice will not have the edge it will have later in the day, nor will it be as limber. Your "morning voice" probably will have more air in it and less bite. But that is to be expected. Don't let this deter you from singing early in the day.

If you have a rehearsal, audition or show scheduled at ten o'clock in the morning, be sure you are up at 7 AM. You will need this time to warm up. Follow the same routine you would use for an evening performance. Remember the importance of deep breathing and panting. Work on your "head voice" and so on.

In addition to warming up for a specific performance on a given day, work on building your vocal stamina before each engagement. This is particularly true if you have had time off and have not been performing. For instance, if you are going to be working in Las Vegas, Reno or any dry, desert area, or if you're going to be working at a high altitude (Denver, Lake Tahoe, Mexico City, etc.), you need to start building your stamina at least a week before the engagement begins. If you will be doing two shows a night, try to sing the equivalent of two shows in rehearsal. Work with your musical director or accompany yourself, but make yourself sing a couple of hours during each stamina-building session. Also at these sessions, try to simulate the movements (especially dancing) that you will be using in your performance. This pre-conditioning of your vocal mechanism, diaphragm and other muscles will enable your body to do what you expect it to do when you get on stage.

Most vocal fatigue is not the result of what you do *during* the engagement, but rather the result of what you didn't do *before* the engagement.

## DRINKING, SMOKING AND DRUGS

As mentioned in Chapter One, it's a good idea to have your vocal chords examined when they are in a normal state. It is also a good idea to avoid excessive use of alcohol, cigarettes, cigars and drugs which may damage your vocal chords and impair your ability to sing.

Our survey shows that, among the singers who responded, two thirds do not smoke cigarettes. One third of those responding said they do smoke. None of the respondents said they drink alcohol every day, although it may be assumed that some drink occasionally. As Americans become increasingly more health conscious, these findings should not be surprising. Nor should it be surprising that 60% of those surveyed said they exercise regularly, while only 40% said they do not.

What are the dangers of using nicotine, alcohol, marijuana and cocaine?

Used excessively, all of these substances can be injurious to your health in general and to your vocal mechanism in particular. The effects of nicotine on health have been studied extensively for many years, and more is known about it than is known about alcohol, marijuana and cocaine. According to Dr. Michael Dennis of Santa Barbara, California, who presently specializes in reconstructive surgery, nicotine (from cigarettes, cigars and pipes) produces a drying effect on the vocal chords, making them more prone to infection, ulcerations and polyps.

Also, according to Dr. Joseph C. Elia of Reno, Nevada, a leading ear, nose and throat specialist, smoking tobacco compromises the ventilation of the lungs with foreign material and destroys the cilia (the tiny appendages on the mucous membrane which lines the lung). This causes the air spaces in the lungs to become less elastic and "clogged" with foreign material. As a result, Dr. Elia points out, the diaphragm does not behave as it should and, without good diaphragmatic action, the singer has greater difficulty producing a sufficient supply of air which is necessary to get the vocal chords vibrating.

But doctors agree the most serious long-term effect of using nicotine is biological. That is, nicotine actually changes the cellular structure of tissues. According to Dr. Dennis, nicotine directly affects the surface lining on the vocal chords and, over a long period of time, causes scarring which eventually makes the chords stiff. Research shows that this process, if allowed to continue, can result in cancer.

Dr. Dennis also notes that the injurious effect of nicotine is cumulative. This means that the vocal chords never forget. If you stop smoking, then start again, the chords are re-injured again as if you never stopped. In addition, smokers generally produce more mucous and, therefore, have to clear their throats more frequently than non-smokers. This clearing of the throat, if done harshly, further irritates and abuses the vocal chords.

Remember that singing requires muscle (the vocal chords) and air (from the lungs and diaphragm), and the tar and nicotine from tobacco smoke has an injurious effect on both. If you use tobacco, some ear, nose and throat doctors recommend that you stick to one brand so that your mucous membranes can become accustomed to the tar and nicotine content of that tobacco. Changing brands, they argue, can further aggravate the already harmful effects of smoking tobacco.

Less is known about the effects of smoking marijuana but, according to Dr. Dennis, physicians who regularly examine the throats and vocal chords of marijuana users believe that inhaling one joint (marijuana cigarette) may be the equivalent of smoking one and a half packs of cigarettes. Whether this is accurate or not, like tobacco, marijuana has a drying effect on the vocal chords and, with prolonged use, can cause the chords to become brittle. Furthermore, as Dr. Elia has pointed out, smoking marijuana can reduce the elasticity of the lungs and impair their ability to force air up the trachea to the vocal chords. While there presently is no evidence that marijuana smoking leads to cancer, some doctors and researchers believe that this could be proven in the future.

Alcohol, if swallowed normally, does not come into contact with the vocal chords. And drinking alcohol, by itself, probably has very little effect on the chords. However, doctors say excessive consumption of alcohol does increase the risk of liver disease and throat cancer. And singers complain that heavy drinking causes dehydration which leaves the vocal chords dry and rough "the morning after." The antidote for this condition would be to drink as much water as possible.

But alcohol is more dangerous when used by tobacco smokers. In medical terminology, alcohol is synergistic with nicotine, which means that the two substances act together to produce a total effect which is greater than that of either one taken separately. The reason for this is that, in most cases, alcohol has the effect of relaxing the tobacco smoker, causing him to inhale the tobacco smoke more deeply.

What are the effects of cocaine on the vocal mechanism? According to Dr. Dennis, when sniffed up the nasal passages, coke acts as a "vaso constrictor," which simply means that it constricts the tiny blood vessels in the nose and limits the blood supply to tissues. He also warns that prolonged use of cocaine leads to ulcerations and, in some cases, perforations in the sceptum (the cartilage which separates the nostrils). Once the sceptum is perforated, you may end up with a "whistling sound" when you breath which obviously could affect your vocal sound. Dr. Elia notes that frequent use of cocaine also compromises the use of the sinuses as resonators.

While it is unlikely that cocaine would have a topical effect on the vocal chords themselves, it is possible, according to Dr. Dennis, that sniffing coke can affect the "false chords" which are located below the vocal chords. These "false chords" are made of a different material than the vocal chords, and cocaine can have a deliterious effect on them, causing them to go into spasms. Such spasms in the "false chords" would affect singing since these chords help the singer to modulate tone.

It also should be pointed out that, while sniffing cocaine may cause the nasal passages to become clear temporarily, the blood vessels and membranes swell back to a larger size than they were before the coke was used, and this can cause nasal congestion and drainage which could affect the vocal sound. Certain types of nose drops and nasal sprays may have a similar effect.

If you use any of these stimulants, remember that, if used excessively, they can be extremely harmful to your voice. In the end, is it worth it?

## COPING WITH VOCAL FATIGUE

No matter how healthy you are or how much vocal stamina you have, you are bound to experience vocal fatigue sometimes. Even if you are living a good, clean life and singing correctly, fatigue can result. In his treatise on "The Care and Treatment of the Singer," presented to a major symposium of South American ear, nose and throat doctors, Dr. Elia has written: "The occupation of the singer is associated with unusual problems, such as illnesses of associates, scanty clothing, responsive audiences demanding encore after encore of a tired and spent singer, unresponsive audiences neither acclaiming nor disclaiming a performance, inhalation of tobacco smoke and other pollutants, unusual working hours, irritation caused by stage lights and makeup, changes in climate, changes in time zones, travel fatigue and new environments. Any of these may contribute to the difficulties which tax the singing apparatus of the performer."

Here are some other common causes for vocal fatigue:

1. *Trying to make your voice sound like someone else's.* You may hear a record that you enjoy and subconsciously try to imitate the singer's vocal sound. Imitating someone else can cause you to strain your voice without even being aware of it.

2. *Strenuous movement on stage.* If you dance or move around a lot on stage, you may strain your voice by failing to give it adequate

support from the diaphragm; you become winded and have too little air left to sing properly.

3. *Singing above your real, usable range.* Remember that just because you can hit a note once in a recording studio or when the conditions are perfect in rehearsal, does not mean you can sustain that note in the excitement of a show, night after night. Barry Manilow, for example, sings in *lower* keys when performing in person than he does on records.

4. *Becoming too excited or overly emotional.* Try not to scream or force emotion into your voice as this, too, can cause vocal strain. Keep in mind that the audience wants to know that you're making some commitment to your vocal performance, but they don't want to feel as though you're straining or hurting yourself.

5. *Faulty Monitors.* If your voice is not loud enough in the on-stage speakers, you may strain your voice trying to sing above the band. Or if the quality of your voice in the monitors is not your natural sound, you subconsciously may compensate by trying to make the sound you're accustomed to hearing. This, too, may lead to vocal strain.

## DANGER SIGNALS

Be aware of the warning symptoms of vocal fatigue and constantly monitor your body and your voice for these symptoms. For instance, one of the first signs of fatigue is when you notice that you're losing volume and edge in your voice. If your voice begins to sound breathier and you are having difficulty hearing yourself over the band, you probably are experiencing vocal fatigue. (One sure sign is when you have to keep asking for more volume in the on-stage vocal monitors.)

When the vocal chords are fatigued, they become swollen and, therefore, do not "approximate" or come together as they should to produce a fine, clear-sounding tone. And if you don't force enough air over the chords, eventually you will become hoarse.

If, after a performance, you feel heat in your throat near your vocal chords, this may be an early sign of infection. See a doctor. If, on the other hand, you have a cold which does not involve your vocal mechanism—a head cold or nasal congestion—you still should be able to sing reasonably well. Of course, your voice will sound differently to you because you won't have the benefit of hearing it through clear, resonating nasal passages.

Be careful when using products such as nasal sprays or pills that "dry up" a cold. These products take away the necessary lubricants around the vocal chords. Your vocal chords need to be moist and, for this reason, many singers use a humidifier at night and in the dressing room when working in desert areas. Others feel you should simply let your vocal mechanism adjust to the climate. If you are going to be working in an unusual climate to which you have not become accustomed, try to arrive a few days in advance to give your body a chance to adapt.

If your vocal chords are fatigued and swollen, the fine edge in your voice usually can be brought back with steam. One easy way to get steam is to fill the bathroom sink with hot (boiling, if possible) water, put a towel over your head (to capture the steam) and place your face just above the water. Inhale deeply. When done two or three times a day, this usually will bring relief. Another source of steam, of course, is a steam room. But, when using a steam room, be careful not to dehydrate your body by staying in too long.

Throat lozenges with menthol don't really reach the vocal chords, but sometimes such lozenges can be helpful in clearing congested nasal passages. The only way to get moisture directly to the chords (that is, topically) is to use an atomizer. This is a temporary measure and is most effective if done just before singing. The mist from the atomizer will help clear dried mucous from the chords and reduce swelling. Larylgyn brand spray is effective, as is the mixture historically used by Vienna opera singers. The Vienna mixture is one-half concentrated lemon juice and one-half adrenal chloride, which is sold over-the-counter in most drug stores without a prescription. Used in an atomizer, the combination of lemon juice and adrenal chloride is harmless and can be used any number of times with no negative side-effects.

In extreme cases of vocal fatigue, your ear, nose and throat specialist may prescribe a cortisone derivative such as Decadron or Medrol. These cortisone derivative drugs temporarily shrink the vocal chords, giving you back the edge in your voice. However, many doctors warn that prolonged use is dangerous and repeated use in any given year can be harmful. Always consult your doctor when there is a vocal problem. Home or hearsay remedies may be harmful.

## HOW TO SING WHEN YOU THINK YOU CAN'T

When all is said and done, even if you are suffering from extreme vocal fatigue, it still is possible—and often essential—to go on and perform anyway. When "the show must go on" and you wish it didn't have to, remember these points:

1. Speak the words to the song using very little sustained vocal tone;
2. Eliminate troublesome high notes by re-phrasing difficult passages;
3. Use lots of air. Don't be afraid to use a breathier sound;
4. Let the microphone do the work for you. It can give you the volume and presence you may not otherwise have;
5. Sell each song as usual. Remember that it is your commitment to the show and your attitude which is most important and most apparent to the audience.

The best medicine for vocal fatigue is a good, positive attitude. Singing, after all, is as much mental as physical. And if you approach your performance with confidence, self-assurance and determination, the audience will respond. Even when you are not at your best vocally, you still must be the best entertainer you can be.

Also, always keep in mind that you will be far more critical of your voice, its strengths and weaknesses, during any given performance than the audience will be. They are judging your total performance, not just your vocal ability. As we have discussed, the audience responds not only to your delivery of material, but also to your choice of material, your energy (pacing and commitment) and, perhaps most importantly, your rapport with them.

Remember this basic assumption: Even when you know you could be singing better, the audience doesn't. The next time you have to sing when you think you can't, keep those words in the back of your mind—they'll never know.

# CHAPTER 8

# RECORDING

*"I don't write songs, I write* records.*"*
*—Neil Diamond*

**Hit records make stars.**

When a record, any record, reaches the Top 10 on the national charts printed each week in *Billboard, Cash Box* and *Record World* magazines, it means at least 500,000 people have walked into record stores and purchased that record.

It means that record is being played at the rate of at least once every hour on every major AM radio station in every major city in the United States.

It means the singer or group who recorded that song is now known by hundreds of thousands of people, perhaps even millions.

It means millions of people have heard the song on their radios, even though they might not have bought the record.

It means millions more eventually may see and hear that song performed on television.

It means the singer or group who made the record is earning tens of thousands of dollars from personal appearances which would not have been booked were it not for that hit record.

It means the artist, the songwriter, the publisher and the record company who put out the record are earning tens of thousands of dollars in royalty payments.

Hit records make the music business go around.

According to *This Business of Music* (Sidney Shemel and M. William Krasilovsky, Billboard Books), there are radios in over 98% of all the homes in the United States and in 95% of all automobiles. Over 73 million stereo systems were in use in 1975. Retail sales of records boomed from $48 million in 1940 to $2.36 *billion* in 1975 to well over $3 *billion* in 1978.

And hit records are the life blood of the singing entertainer. If we are not making them, then we are singing them. Thus, learning the art, craft and business of recording is of paramount importance in every singing career.

The best way to learn about recording is to make demos, relatively inexpensive demonstration tapes, which sell you as a singer and, if you write, as a songwriter. Demos also are the best way to present yourself to music publishers, entertainment buyers, agents, managers and record companies.


## DEMONSTRATION RECORDS

When you're starting out, no one is going to take your word for it that you could be the next big singing sensation. You have to prove yourself—on tape. You can get jobs by auditioning in person, and if you are a songwriter looking for a publishing deal, sometimes you can get an appointment to sing live at a piano or with a guitar in the office. (If the publisher likes what he hears, he may even record you in his own studio or lay out a few dollars to pay for piano or guitar and voice demos.) But for the most part, record companies, agents, managers and music publishers simply don't have time to audition every band or singer who comes to their attention.

Every music business executive worth his vinyl has a tape recorder in his office, and it takes only a few minutes to thread a tape machine and listen to a demo. A good demo, furthermore, shows not only how well you sing and play, but also how well you record. Record companies and music publishers listen for originality and commercial potential. If they like your demo, they may want to come see you perform live. And if they still like you, your tape may be submitted at the next talent acquisition meeting. (Most talent scouts and lower-level record company people don't have the power to sign acts to the label.) The next step could be making two or four "masters", the high quality recordings from which records are made. The record company pays for the masters and, if they like the way they turn out, they may put two of the masters together to make a single (i.e., 45 rpm) record. If your single then is released and does reasonably well, you could be on your way to making your first album (usually made up of ten masters). This type of record deal is called a "singles deal." Because they involve less money and, therefore, less financial risk for the record company, "singles deals" are becoming increasingly popular.

Making demos is important for other reasons. Going into the studio on your own to make a demo enables you to learn first hand about the recording process and it gives you the opportunity to make mistakes at a time when no one in the business is paying much attention to your career. Because making demos is relatively inexpensive, you can afford to make several until you have one or two which you think best reflect your particular talent. Another reason for making demos is they allow you to present yourself in the best possible light, whereas in live auditions–singing in an office is particularly awkward and difficult– you undoubtedly will be more nervous and have less control over the performing environment.

## WHAT TO RECORD

By definition, what singing entertainers do is perform well-known material and, in that sense, the singing entertainer is a mirror for society. But when it comes to recording, the singing entertainer must shed his role as a mirror and become instead an innovator or, ideally, a trend-setter. In recording, it is imperative to be an original, never a copy. Whether you're making your first demo or your first album, you must create, not imitate. It does no good to record songs that already have been recorded, except in very rare instances.

There was a time, however, when the record companies, especially Columbia Records, strongly encouraged certain kinds of recording artists to record the popular hits of the day, songs which had been made popular by other singers or groups. Many artists such as Johnny Mathis, Robert Goulet, Jack Jones, Andy Williams, Jerry Vale, John Davidson and Dean Martin were in this category. The theory then was that fans wanted to hear their favorite singers sing the most popular songs of the time. Hence, you had Andy Williams singing "Yesterday," made famous by The Beatles, or Dean Martin singing "Gentle On My Mind," made popular by Glen Campbell. This formula later proved to be bankrupt and very few contemporary recording artists continue to adhere to it. Nowadays, according to music publisher Al Gallico, established artists only record popular hits if they need to fill-out an album of original and/or unknown songs which have the potential of becoming hits. Most American record buyers clearly prefer buying the original, not an imitation.

There are very few hard and fast rules about recording. But if there is one rule which should be observed by every singer, especially when you are first starting to record demos, it is never record currently popular hits or songs which have been major hits in the last five years. The purpose of a demo is to sell you as a singer who has commercial potential as a recording artist. Recording currently popular hit songs, even though they may show off your vocal abilities, is a waste of time and money, for they do not demonstrate that you may be capable of coming up with a hit record on your own.

The only time it is advisable to record well-known material is when you want to make a presentation tape for entertainment buyers. In most cases, though, a live recording made while you are working will suffice for this purpose. If you're going to spend the money and the time to go into a recording studio, record unknown songs, unfamiliar songs, undiscovered songs, original songs or old hits ("oldies") which have not yet been re-recorded or re-released. This way you will have something original which you can submit to record companies and publishers, and which also will be impressive to buyers, agents and managers.

When choosing unknown, obscure or original material for a demo, apply the same criterion as you would for picking well-known material (see Chapter Three). That is, except for the fact that the song should *not* be familiar, it should be a song which has broad audience appeal; and it should be a song with which you can identify strongly as a singer.

The most commercial songs are simply constructed. They use parallel phrases, singable, repetitious and, therefore, memorable melodies and catchy or thought-provoking lyrics. Some of the most common types of hit songs are story songs, love ballads, rhythm or "groove" songs and songs with strong, identifiable instrumental signatures. A story song usually is a simply constructed song which has a readily memorable and singable chorus. Good examples are Vicki Lawrence's version of "Rainy Night In Georgia," Jimmy Dean's "Big Bad John" and Kenny Rogers' "Lucille." Love ballads must be extremely well-crafted songs which either are so simple in construction or so unique lyrically that they have immediate impact. Examples of powerful love ballads are "I Honestly Love You" (Olivia Newton-John), "Behind Closed Doors" (Charlie Rich) and "Just The Way You Are" (Billy Joel). Rhythm or "groove" songs make it primarily because of their infectious, high energy or their hypnotic mood. "I Want To Kiss You All Over" and "Some Kind of Wonderful" are examples of "groove" songs. A strong instrumental hook also can make a song more commercial, such as in the Jerry Rafferty song, "Baker Street," where the saxophone solo became the most recognizable element in the record.

We can't emphasize enough the importance of selecting the right songs when you're recording. Arrangements, production, even musicianship are secondary. The success of a recording ultimately depends on the worthiness of the material. If a song is not powerful, unique or otherwise captivating, no amount of production gimmickery will make it a successful recording. In the words of Tony Orlando, "People don't buy performances. They don't buy charts (i.e., arrangements). They buy *songs.* That's the name of the game in this business."

Furthermore, keep in mind when you are choosing and routining songs for recording, they should, in most cases, be no longer than 2½ to 3 minutes. Try to make even your demos sound as much as possible like records that could be played on the radio. Of course, it is unlikely that your demos ever will get any airplay, but still it is wise to force yourself to work within the limitations applied to commercial records. Record songs that could be *singles.* Don't record filler-type songs or album cuts. If your first song doesn't grab the listener in the first eight bars or so, the rest of your demo tape may never be heard.

## SEARCHING FOR SONGS

Where can you find songs to record?

Call music publishers and tell them you are going into the studio to make a demo. Ask each publisher if he has any *new* songs which he needs "demoed." Say that you'll pay for the demo if he'll allow you to record the song, and offer the publisher a copy of the finished product. Be sure to explain that you are not making a record for commercial release, but rather a demo to present yourself as an artist. One note of caution: never *pay* a publisher for the privilege of recording one of his songs.

If you don't write songs yourself, try to meet songwriters. There are thousands of them around. Cultivate a relationship with a writer whose songs you like and try to get first crack at making demos of his or her songs. (Many songwriters do not wish to record their own songs, and they are grateful to find a competent singer who is willing to do so.)

Listen to albums for good, commercial songs which may have gone undiscovered. Kris Kristofferson's song, "Me and Bobby McGee" was recorded by several artists on several albums before it became a big hit for Janis Joplin. Generally, when listening to albums, you are better off concentrating on albums by songwriters (or groups) who write their own material. And you're more likely to find songs to demo on older albums; chances are the songs on newer albums already have been or are being considered for release as singles if they are strong enough.

Write your own songs. There is no question that being a songwriter makes you more desirable to record companies, for it gives you a built-in source of material. Equally important is the fact that songwriting gives you immediate claim to your material which the non-writing singer does not have. And it also should be pointed out that one of the best ways to become a recording artist yourself is to first write a hit song for someone else. Paul Williams, Paul Anka, Carole King, Neil Sedaka and Neil Diamond are examples of songwriters who later became recording artists.

## RECORD PRODUCERS

What about a producer? When you're first starting to make demos, you probably don't need a producer per se. In the beginning, a musical director, arranger or the musician who is the leader of the session can serve as your "producer." Also, in many cases, the studio engineer can fill this role. Once you have a recording contract, however, and often as a condition for getting one, a producer is essential. Every artist ultimately needs someone who can help choose material, organize recording sessions and see to it that your best performances get on tape. As the artist, there is no way you can be on both sides of the glass at the same time. A producer who has the perspective of the audience, that is, the record-buying public, will be able to evaluate more objectively what you do in the studio as well as make constructive criticisms and suggestions. But in the early going before you have a record deal, it may be difficult to get an established record producer interested in your career. Don't let this discourage you. Go ahead and put together your first few demo sessions yourself. Demo-making is a learning process.

## PREPARING TO GO INTO THE STUDIO

In Chapter Three we discussed routining songs. Before you go into the recording studio, routine the songs you are going to record. But this time, routine each song to be a *record.* Be sure you have an ear-catching introductory instrumental lick. Be sure the first line in the lyric draws the listener in. To accomplish this, the first line, indeed the first verse has to be strong lyrically and melodically; and your delivery has to seduce the listener. It has to be a compelling vocal. Remember that an effective demo should grab the listener immediately and never let him go for 2½ to 3 minutes.

After you've routined the song(s) you're going to record, you, your musical director or an arranger should prepare lead sheets for all of the musicians you will be using on the session. These lead sheets do not have to be intricate or complicated; simple chord charts and lyric sheets will be sufficient. If there is any confusion or a dispute about any chord or lyric, having "charts" will save time.

Now you're ready to rehearse your musicians and singers. This should be done *outside* the studio. Call the musicians together some-where—rent a rehearsal hall or use your garage—and run through each song with the band. Make changes where necessary and encourage the musicians to contribute their musical ideas. Once the band has re-hearsed, rehearse the background singers. This is when they should work out their harmony parts, entrances and exits in the song.

*Never rehearse in the studio.* You, your musicians and your singers should be completely prepared before you get to the studio. When the clock is running in the studio—which means you're spending money—you should be recording, not practicing. If you use professional studio musicians instead of your own band, you will not rehearse before the session. These musicians will read your lead sheets perfectly and may even make suggestions that will save valuable studio time. Otherwise, you must rehearse in advance.

Singers often wonder how far they should go in producing demos. As Kenny Rogers and Len Epand have pointed out in their book, *Making*

*It With Music* (Harper & Row), there are two schools of thought. Many music people prefer to hear sparsely produced demos where the bare essentials are clear—the melody, the lyric, the singer's vocal ability and an instrumental. This is the "old school" way which appeals to people who like to imagine what *they* can do to enhance the singer or band in terms of sound and production. Others are spoiled. They are used to hearing elaborately produced demos—some singers spend as much as $10,000 on what end up being "super demos," if not masters—and anything less may be a disappointment. They leave nothing to the imagination. But as Rogers and Epand wisely recommend, "The answer isn't to spend ten grand on a demo. Seek a middle ground, keeping the recording full-sounding but uncluttered. Season it with just the tastiest of your production ideas, ideas that enhance the songs and add to the band's (or singer's) distinctiveness."

An effective demo can be made using a four-piece band—piano, bass, drums and guitar. Instruments such as steel guitar, horns or keyboard strings (Arp or Moog synthesizer) can be added after the basic rhythm tracks have been made. And three background singers can add a lot of body and texture to a simple demo without making it sound over-produced.

## WORKING IN THE STUDIO

Once you have routined your songs *as records* and rehearsed them with your band and singers, call several recording studios and compare their prices. Don't necessarily choose the cheapest studio. Try to find a reasonably priced studio which is set up to do demo recordings. Be sure the studio has the equipment you need. In addition to recording equipment and mikes, does the studio have a piano, organ, synthesizer or other instruments you may require? Inquire about the charges, if any, for using these instruments. Talk to the recording engineer, if you can, and explain to him or her exactly what you are trying to do. If the engineer sounds knowledgeable, cooperative and enthusiastic and the price is fair, book that studio. Now, put together a budget. Often, it is possible to hire musicians for demos (not records) for $20 to $25 per song. (In some cases, you may have to pay musicians applicable Union scale for demos.) The studio will charge you for recording and mixing time, recording tape and, in some cases, for the use of certain studio instruments. (Normally, you should not have to pay extra for the use of a piano.) Make an allowance in the budget for the cost of lead sheets and tape copying, and set aside a few extra dollars in a contingency fund for costs you may not have anticipated.

Don't take a lot of extraneous people to the studio. The studio is a place to work, not party; everyone at your session should have a reason for being there. The more professional your attitude, the more likely you are to get a professional-sounding demo. You can have a party *after* the session.

A demo recording can be made on anything from a two-track to a 16 or 24-track recording machine. Recording 16-track or 24-track can cost upwards of $125 an hour, however, and isn't necessary in the beginning. In fact, some musicians feel that 16 and 24-track recording in inexperienced hands can be harmful in that it inevitably leads to overproduction. Two-track recording, on the other hand, is useful only for making piano or guitar-voice demos. Ideally, you should make your first demos in either a four-track or eight-track studio. Such studios typically have sound mixing boards capable of receiving the in-put from eight to 16 microphones, more than enough to mike a four-piece band. The engineer can control the volume and E.Q. (bass, treble, midrange) for each microphone and "mix" them down, i.e., place each in its proper perspective. The "mix" then is fed to the four or eight tracks on the recording machine.

Visualize an eight-channel mixing board and a four-track recording machine. The board may be set up as follows:

Channel 1 - Lead vocal
Channel 2 - Bass
Channel 3 - Kick (Bass) Drum
Channel 4 - Overhead Drums

Channel 5 - Rhythm guitar
Channel 6 - Piano
Channel 7 - Background vocals
Channel 8 - Background vocals, doubled, or a solo instrument

When recording on a four-track machine, these eight channels (inputs) must be combined in some manner and sent (out-put) to the four recording tracks. The recording engineer can decide the best way to do this.

For example, the lead vocal (Channel 1), which you may wish to re-record several times until you get it the way you want it, can go on Track 1 of the tape. Bass, drums, rhythm guitar and piano (Channels 2-6) can be combined ("sub-mixed") and put on Track 2. Background vocals (Channel 7) can go onto Track 3, and the "doubled" (exactly repeated) background vocals or a solo instrument can go on the remaining track, Track 4. (See diagram pg. 176.)

The recording engineer might set up the board differently. But the main thing to remember when recording in a four-track studio is to keep your lead vocal on a separate track by itself. If need be, you can combine bass, drums, piano and rhythm guitar(s) onto one track, making what is called the "rhythm track." But keep your lead vocal, background vocals and any solo instruments on separate tracks so that later, when you mix down the four tracks to make a stereo "final mix," they can be brought up without bringing up the volume of the other instruments and vocals. Be sure the engineer never puts your lead vocal on the same track with drums or bass, for if you want more vocal in the mix, you'll be stuck with getting more bass and drums with it.

Recording in an eight-track studio provides even more flexibility and, obviously, reduces the need to combine tracks. With eight tracks, all the instruments and vocals can be recorded at once on separate tracks on tape and "mixed down" later. You can record the rhythm track, and then the engineer can replay it for, say, the lead guitarist until he gets his part down. This then can be replayed while the background singers add their parts. Finally, the tape can be played until you get a lead vocal performance which you like. The advantage here is, each new

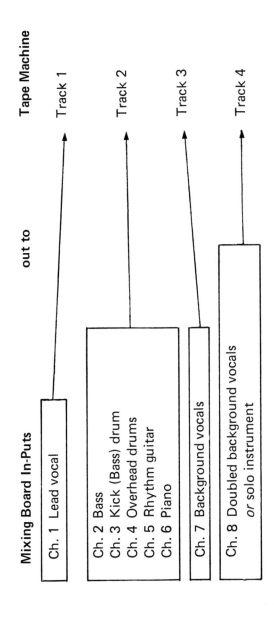

addition (called "over-dubs") is made by playing with the tape, not the band. Studios offering eight-track equipment charge from $25 to $40 an hour for studio time (the cost of tape always is extra). Don't be afraid to bargain with the studio owner or manager. If you are willing to record early in the day or very late at night, often the studio will give you a break on their regular rate. Once you establish a good relationship with a studio and engineer, give that studio all of your demo business. In turn, they probably will throw in a few "free" hours.

Wherever the cost of recording four-track is comparable to recording eight-track, you should record eight-track. Even if it costs a little more, the advantages of eight-track recording make it the preferable way to go. Insist that microphones and other equipment be set up *prior* to the starting time for your recording session. When you arrive at the studio, plan on spending the first 15 minutes of the session getting a sound balance.

The engineer will direct you as to the best way to arrange your musicians and equipment, and he or she will place the mikes and set up the mixing board. Once this is done, run down the first song with the band. Try in the first 30 minutes of recording to get at least one, complete performance or "take" of the song. This should be no problem if you have rehearsed in advance, and it shows the musicians and the engineer that you're a professional. Be business-like in the studio, but try not to let the recording environment intimidate you. Recording should be a satisfying and enjoyable experience, especially if you have good material and are well-prepared. There is nothing more rewarding than starting with a concept for a song and building it into a recording which takes on dimensions of its own. The pressures of working in the studio can be intense; you must be as efficient and yet as relaxed as possible. If you are prepared and confident, you will get what you want.

*Never go into the studio hoping you'll get lucky.* Successful recording is 90% preparation and 10% luck or inspiration.

Psychologically, it is important each time you go into the studio to achieve your goal for that session. If you want to record three songs in three hours—a reasonable goal if you have rehearsed in advance—then pace the session in such a way as to get a good, useable "takc" of all three songs. The way to do this is to learn to judge a good "take" when you hear it, and then move on to the next song. A good "take" may not be flawless, but if it is cohesive and gets the point across—if it *feels* right—save it and move along. Many times, singers will waste time trying to get a better "take" when, in fact, they already have the best performance they're going to get for that session. Remember you're making demos, not masters. Try to sense when the band has reached its peak in playing a given song, capture that peak on tape and then tackle the next one. This is important for a couple of reasons: You'll get three songs recorded instead of one or two; and everyone will leave the studio with a feeling of accomplishment and fulfillment.

Two warnings about working in the studio. Sometimes when you get home, your recording doesn't sound as good to you as it did in the studio. Usually, this is because you've become accustomed to hearing your songs played back in the studio over high-performance studio speakers at a high volume. If you don't have a comparable system at home, somehow the tapes seem less impressive. To compensate for this, ask the studio engineer to play back your songs at a low volume through small speakers such as those found in a tape recorder or car radio. Most studios are equipped to do this. At a lower volume over small speakers, you will get a better idea of how your tape will sound under ordinary circumstances. Also, this is a good way to check the "mix" to make sure the lead vocal is loud enough—don't let the engineer bury your vocal in the track—and the instruments are in proper perspective.

Another thing to be aware of in the studio is "tired ears." After several hours of listening to music played back at high volume levels, your ears literally become exhausted. You may notice during the session that with each successive play-back, the engineer is increasing the play-back volume. Your ears are loosing their capacity to hear all the highs and lows. If this happens to you, take a break or ask the engineer to reduce volume levels to give your ears a chance to rest. If necessary, wait to do "final mixes" of your songs when your ears are "fresh."

## MAKING COPIES AND SUBMITTING TAPES

When you've finished making your demos, don't have copies made immediately. Play the tunes at home for awhile. Live with the songs. Be sure you are happy with your performance and the "mix." Then, when you're sure you want to use the demos, have copies made. Ordinarily, copies can be made at the studio where you record. Reel-to-reel tape copies should be quarter-track stereo, which means they can be played on most office and home tape decks. Cassette copies should be made on high quality cassettes. They may cost a few dollars more, but it's worth it. After all, you've already spent your hard-earned money on making a quality recording. Don't throw away your investment by making copies on cheap tape.

Most record companies and music publishers still prefer reel-to-reel tapes, although cassettes are becoming increasingly popular. It's probably six of one, half a dozen of the other. Have both made and ask whomever you're submitting a tape to which is preferred. Even good quality cassettes do not offer the quality of reproduction possible on reel-to-reel copies, but the difference is so minimal as to not be of concern.

When submitting tapes to record companies or publishers, *never put more than three songs on a tape.* Under office listening conditions, most music business executives have an attention span of about 10 minutes or three songs. After that, they begin to tune out. If they like what they hear, then you may be asked to submit another tape. In this case, submit three more songs. Always put what you think is the catchiest, most commercial song first on the tape. If the first song doesn't get the listener's attention, the others may never be heard. Start with a high energy, up-tempo song, put your ballad in the middle, and finish with another up-tempo selection.

Allow at least a week for a record company A & R (artists and repertoire) person or music publisher to listen to your tape. If you haven't heard anything in ten days, call the office and ask if your tape has been heard. If the record company or publisher "passes" on your tape (the euphemism for rejecting it), ask them to return it. Always put your name, address and phone number on the tape or cassette box and include a stamped (third class), self-addressed return envelope with every submission. If you have a good picture of yourself (preferably performing), send it along with your tape. But if you don't have good pictures, it's better to let the listener wonder what you look like. Who knows, maybe you'll be invited to come into the office just so they can have a look at you.

Don't be discouraged if someone "passes" on your tape and sends it back to you. It doesn't mean you can't interest them with your next tape. In the beginning, rejection is part of the process of learning how to record. The singer who makes it is the singer who refuses to give up and, instead, concentrates on trying to make each demo better than the one before.

Also, if you can develop any sort of personal contact within a record company or a publisher's office, this makes submitting your tapes easier. Don't be afraid to call the record company A & R department and ask who listens to tapes by new artists. At least then you'll have the name of a person to whom you can send your tape and a person you can call later for a reaction. If you have a musical director, arranger, producer, manager or agent who has record company or publishing company contacts, use them. It is far better to submit a tape through someone you know or to someone you have just met than to send it completely unsolicited through the mail.

If you include lyric sheets with your tape, be sure they are legibly typed and easy to follow. If you write a covering letter to accompany the tape, make it brief and to the point. Simply say, "I would appreciate it if you would listen to my tape and take a few minutes to let me know what you think of it." Whatever you write, don't explain the songs, don't apologize for the quality of the recording (if it's not good quality, don't submit it) and don't offer a lot of unnecessary biographical information about yourself. The test of a good demo is in the listening. If the tape doesn't say it, a letter won't help.

Do not make a pest of yourself. Record company executives, publishers, agents and managers constantly are deluged with tapes. Be patient. Realize that it's going to take some time before they get to yours. Conduct yourself in a courteous, professional manner at all times. If you have included a stamped, self-addressed return envelope with your submission and have made a couple of follow-up calls, you'll get an answer and/or your tape back soon enough.

If you should be fortunate enough to get a record company or a music publisher interested in what you do, take a few hours to read the appropriate chapters in *This Business of Music* pertaining to recording and publishing deals, advances and royalty payments. There is no more complete compendium of information available on these and many other related subjects. Also, if you should be offered a recording or publishing deal, do not sign it until you have had it reviewed by an attorney familiar with such deals and have read it yourself. Contracts and agreements often are not as complicated as they may seem. If you don't understand a particular provision, or if the language is unclear, ask for clarification. Don't be pressured into signing anything without first reading "the fine print." *And never pay a record company to record you.* That's not how business is done. If money is to change hands, you should be the one receiving it.


## THE ART OF RECORDING

Unquestionably, there is an art to recording successfully. You must learn how to give a good *record* performance, which is different than giving a good live performance. Over 80% of the singers surveyed for this book said they sing differently when making a record than they do in front of an audience. Most of those surveyed said they are "more conscious of each note" they sing when recording; many said they sing more softly in the studio than they do on stage; and the majority indicated they "concentrate more on feeling and sound." Some, including Barry Manilow, said they sing in higher keys when recording. Bette Midler said, "One is always more careful when it's for posterity."

Making a record is, in a sense, making history. Your vocal performance must be able to stand the test of time. It must be a vocal which holds up listening after listening. And it must be a performance which touches the listener solely by its sound and feeling, for the listener does not have the benefit of seeing the performer.

Many accomplished and otherwise successful singers have had difficulty developing an effective, commercial recording style. While their live performances may be outstanding, their recording careers have been limited.

In the "cool" medium of recording (see Chapter Six), a vocal performance which is too intense, too "hot" in the McLuhan sense, and not evocative enough in a subtle way, is not a good recording vocal. When asked if he sings louder in person than in the recording studio, Kenny Rogers, who won a Grammy award in 1978 for his hit, "Lucille," replied: "I sing softly all the time." By doing so, Rogers explains, he can concentrate on getting the feeling and the little emotional nuances in his voice which make for a compelling vocal performance in person or on record. Neil Diamond is another singer who has an effective, unique and commercial vocal sound for recording. And, like Rogers, it is a sound which he seems to be able to duplicate effortlessly on stage.

Recording has become the pop singer's most important tool. In Al Jolson's day, recording merely was a way of capturing a live performance. It was a means to an end. Today, however, recording is an end unto itself. That is, we don't record simply to capture a live performance; we record to create a separate and distinct kind of performance—a recorded performance. To be a successful recording artist in today's market, you must sing in the studio as if you're singing to one person who is sitting right in front of you with his eyes closed. Your goal is to reach that person strictly through the sound of your voice and all that it encompasses.

Al Jolson was not successful at this. Bing Crosby, on the other hand, was, and he took the recording world by storm because he was capable of making records that sounded like he was singing intimately, one-to-one. Even today, many great live performers overwhelm the microphone in the recording studio. To use the terminology we used in Chapter Six, they confuse *intensity* with *intent.*

On record, the singer's intensity must be minimized and intent must be magnified. For a recorded performance, you must not project too much. You must do a smaller, more subtle performance. Every nuance still will come across.

As you reduce the size of your performance—as you focus it—you must keep your intent the same or increase it. The emotion you convey no longer is a factor of volume or intensity, as it is on stage. In recording, emotion and feeling are conveyed strictly by the sound you produce. A light, airy, high vocal sound conveys innocence. A crack in the voice conveys pain or vulnerability. And, when recording, a little goes a long way. A large, resonating (loud) stage voice, when recorded, sounds dishonest, because the listener gets the impression the singer is performing beyond the medium. The performance doesn't sound like it's for him. It doesn't sound intimate.

The vocal on a record should excite or lure in the listener. It can't be a safe, non-committal vocal. It has to move organs. Remember that the medium of recording is an *aural* (audio) medium. Straight teeth, good hair, smart clothes, fancy dancing and sparkling eyes don't come across on a vinyl disc. The ears are the judge and jury. Listen to any of the singers who have become successful recording artists and try to figure out what qualities in their voices, or in their phrasing make them effective on record. Listen to your own demos this way. Naturally, it is difficult to be objective about your own voice, especially until you have heard your recorded voice many times. But as you go along, you will be able to be more objective. Ask yourself if your vocal is believable. Is it sincere? Does it communicate? Even though it may be technically flawed in spots, does it have real feeling? Is it a voice that draws you in as a listener? Is it an interesting voice? Does it have character? Does it sound natural?

Granted, these are difficult questions to answer. Your friends, musical director, producer and recording engineer are in a better position to be objective judges about these things. Nevertheless, these are the crucial questions which must be asked every time you sing in the studio.

Some final notes about recording. No one yet has come up with a fool-proof formula for making hit records. If there were such a thing, the person who invented it would be a billionaire. To some extent, recording is a matter of trial and error. Also, a hit record involves the successful combination of a number of things. The song must be right, and the singer must be right for the song. The way the record is produced must enhance both song and singer. The record company also must get behind the record and promote it. And you have to get lucky. Anyone who's ever had a hit will tell you that.

So, start learning by making demos. Then make records. And good luck.

# CHAPTER 9

# SELLING YOURSELF

*"I don't make stars. I don't believe*
*any manager really makes stars.* Talent
*makes stars."*
— *Jerry Weintraub,*
*Management III*

**Congratulations!** You're in business for yourself. As a singing entertainer, you're the Chairman of the Board, your own biggest investor and the chief executive in charge of making your career happen.

Now, what are you going to do?

You must take charge. You must become the driving force behind your career. No one cares as much about your career as you do. Even though eventually you may hire others to sell you (agents), personally represent you (managers) and handle public relations for you (press agents), the impetus for your career begins with you. If you're going to be in business for yourself, you must plunge into the business of making yourself a commercial commodity. If you don't, no one else will.

How, then, should you go about getting your business off the ground?

## BECOMING SELF-CONTAINED MUSICALLY

Already we have discussed what you must do to lay the basic foundation for such an enterprise. Before you open your doors to customers, you must package your product—you. You must become an accomplished singer and musician. You must find a musical director who can help you define what you do best. This should be someone who has similar musical tastes as well as someone in whom you have trust. Together, you must choose material, and you must determine how you are going to approach that material. And, ultimately, you must become a self-contained musical entity.

Becoming self-contained musically means you must put together a band which will enable you to work. It no longer is possible for singers to go out and find an orchestra, a band or a trio to sing in front of as it was, say, in the late '40s. Nowadays, you already must have your own accompaniment. This is particularly true when it comes to working in most hotels, restaurants and lounges where it is easier and less expensive for management to hire already-existing packages of singer(s) and musicians.

You may be able to get work without having a band if you are capable of accompanying yourself. Otherwise, except for an occasional audition where you might have the use of an audition piano player, you must have at least one accompanist of your own (another important reason for having a musical director). As a general rule, if you are not self-contained musically, you simply are not employable as a singer in today's market.

Of course, it is true that, from time to time, established musical groups advertise for singers to replace members who have left. However, this generally is not the kind of opportunity which will allow you to further your own particular singing career. Instead, you'll be required to sing whatever type of music has made the group popular and, while this may not be bad experience, eventually it is bound to prove unfulfilling. It also is true that once you become somewhat established as a singing entertainer, you may have opportunities to sing in front of the kind of orchestras which provide accompaniment on television talk shows ("The Tonight Show" orchestra, for example). Or, if you are working in the main room of a major casino-hotel in Las Vegas, Reno or Lake Tahoe, you may be able to augment your own band with the "house band." But these are exceptions rather than the rule.

Shannon Green, a successful, young booking agent in the San Francisco Bay Area who has as many as 20 to 30 acts working in hotel lounges and restaurants each week, told us the "competitive nature of the nightclub business makes it imperative" that a singer be self-contained musically. According to Green, "For every singer *without* a band, there are ten singers *with* bands already rehearsed, ready to play. Entertainment is a relatively small part of the total picture in most hotels and restaurants; management is looking for the most economical way to go—which is booking self-contained acts."

## HIRING & PAYING MUSICIANS

Clearly then, in order to get your first job, you must assemble a band. It may consist of only two musicians, or it may be larger. Obviously, the fewer musicians you have, the more money you will make, especially when you're starting out and not able to command big fees. A singer with two musicians behind him or her is referred to by booking agents as a "one plus two" group, meaning one singer and two back-up musicians. A "one plus four" is a singer backed by four musicians, and a "two plus two" would be a duo backed by two musicians.

Finding musicians shouldn't be a problem. The number of musicians has grown from one in six to one in four Americans in the last eight years, according to a poll conducted by the American Music Conference (*Los Angeles Times,* November 30, 1978). That translates to some 35 million people who have more than a basic knowledge of piano or guitar, the most popular instruments. And yet, when you set out to put a band together, for some reason, it's always hard to find the right musicians. The best way to meet musicians is through friends in the music business. Spread the word that you're looking and, chances are, before long you'll start getting calls. An inexpensive ad in a local newspaper or in music trade papers, local and national, also can be effective. And, of course, you can go to the local office of the American Federation of Musicians (AF of M).

Let's say you want to put together a basic rhythm section—piano, guitar, bass and drums. Interview each of the musicians first. Ask them if they have had any previous professional experience and, if so, with whom and under what circumstances. From this, you can get an idea of which musicians are the most experienced, and you can get a feeling for what they are like as people. A good rule of thumb is to select your musicians based not only on how well they play, but also on their personality, creativity and willingness to work hard. Try to pick people you can relate to socially (you'll be spending a lot of time together) as well as musically, and try to select musicians who get along well with each other (you've got enough problems; you don't need internal dissension). When in doubt, go with the musician who has the most professional attitude and is most dedicated. After all, you need cohesive backing, not virtuoso players or prima donnas.

If you already have a musical director, he or she probably plays piano, so you've got that covered. Look for a bass player and a drummer who have worked together, for they are the basis on which a solid rhythm section is built. When choosing a drummer and bass player, don't be dazzled by technique. In the case of both instruments, often the more simply the instrument is played, the better. Your drummer and bassist should have a good, working knowledge of their respective instruments, be able to keep steady, reliable time and be capable of playing a variety of styles. A good guitar player is one who plays the kinds of "licks" *you* like to hear. Your guitarist also should be experienced in a variety of musical styles, have a good sense of time and know when *not to play* so that arrangements don't become too cluttered.

You will find that the most difficult thing about keeping a band together is money. Musicians need to make a living, too. If you can keep them working, generally they will stay around. If too many weeks, or certainly months, go by without work and a paycheck, you can kiss your band good-bye, which is not the end of the world, by the way. It just means you'll have to put together another band. All singers go through this. And the only way to avoid it is to try to keep working on a regular basis. Later on, when you know you're going to be working a certain number of weeks each year, it's a good idea to put your musicians on a retainer, that is, a guaranteed, annual salary so that you know they'll be there whenever you need them.

Also later on, when you're making lots of money, you may wish to augment your basic rhythm section with the addition of background singers, additional musicians or dancers. In the early stages of your career, however, this is not necessary, and when the time comes, this is a decision your manager can help you make.

It's difficult to say how much you should pay your musicians. In the beginning, particularly if they feel you have some promise as a singer and performer, your musicians should be willing to work for as little as $25 each a night. If you are a "one plus four," this means you've got to be making at least $125 a night to pay the band and yourself equally. You'd have to work five nights a week for everyone (including you) to make $125 a week, which isn't very much given today's rate of inflation. But it's not a terrible place to start. As you progress, your musicians should make a fair wage, either applicable Union scale or more, depending on the economics of the situation. It is not unreasonable for musicians to expect $300 to $400 a week for in-town "gigs" (engagements) and more for going out of town. Some studio musicians working out of Los Angeles make as much as $2,500 to $3,000 a week when they go on the road. The point is, musicians are essential to your business and they should be treated accordingly. If they know that, as you make more money, they also will make more money, there's a good chance the members of your band will stand by you through the lean times.

Paying musicians who already are on your payroll for rehearsal usually is not necessary. If rehearsal is a requirement for getting a job, and you end up getting the job, most musicians won't demand rehearsal pay. When you're first getting started, everyone understands you don't have a lot of money. Ideally, you're better off finding musicians who think of rehearsal as a necessary part of the job and, therefore, are willing to rehearse without receiving additional pay. Just keep in mind that no one can be expected to rehearse forever without receiving some financial reward, either in the form of a job which pays reasonably well or a few dollars for his time and effort.


## GETTING YOUR FIRST JOB

Now, you're ready to get your first job. But how do you get it?

You've got to hustle. You've got to go to every nightclub, restaurant and lounge in your area that hires live entertainment (preferably bands and singers who do what you do) and talk personally to the manager or entertainment buyer. Don't wait for an agent to do this for you. For the most part, agents only are interested in acts which already are working. *You've got to get your first job yourself.*

Dress up, but not too much. Look creative but responsible. Walk in and ask to speak to the manager or entertainment buyer. Introduce yourself, state your business and ask the manager or buyer if he or she has time to talk. If not, ask when you may come back. Be positive, be charming, be persuasive and let the manager or buyer know you mean business, in this case, literally. Restaurants and lounges hire singers and bands for two reasons—to sell drinks and to sell more drinks. So, your job is to convince the manager or buyer that (a) you and your band are professionals; (b) you understand the business; and (c) you are capable of keeping customers in the place, drinking and having a good time, so everyone will be happy. Remember that entertainment in restaurants and lounges is only one aspect of the overall operation of a restaurant or hotel. You must be willing to adapt to the needs of the room you are playing. If management requests that you change some part of your act, try to be accomodating. If you are asked to play your music at a lower volume early in the evening so as not to disturb those who are dining, do so. When you go to work in a restaurant or lounge, you are entering a closed, political system in which there is an established hierarchy. You will be dealing with people who have egos, too, and they will want to feel they can exercise some control over you. This is only natural. After all, to them you are not a "star," but rather another employee.

Be particularly careful to cultivate good relationships with waiters, waitresses and bartenders. At this point in your career, they can help make you or break you.

Kenny Rogers has said that when he first was starting out in Houston, Texas, he used to drive a white Cadillac around town to call on club owners and managers when he was looking for work. One day, Kenny's mother asked him why he had wasted his money on such a fancy car. She thought he ought to get rid of it and save his money for something more important. But Kenny had a good reason for driving that white Cadillac around. He explained, "I'm going into these clubs and asking them to pay me what I consider to be a lot of money and, if they see me drive up in this car, they'll figure somebody else is paying me this kind of money and I must be worth it."

Psychology is important when you're looking for work. You shouldn't appear to be too hungry. You should look reasonably successful. (If you look too successful, they might think you don't need the work.) You shouldn't beg for the job, but you should ask for it. (You'll never get a definite "yes" or "no" unless you come right out and ask for the job.)

You probably will have to audition to get your first few jobs. The club manager or entertainment buyer will set up a time, usually in the late afternoon, when you can come in to the club and perform. For live auditions, put together an "audition set," a selection of songs which shows off what you do in your act. Your "audition set" should be no longer than 30 minutes and, often, a fast-moving, varied 15-minute "set" will do. Your objective in an audition should be to demonstrate that you know how to handle yourself on stage and are capable of singing a variety of contemporary songs in a well-paced show. Even though the club probably will be empty when you audition, except for the owner, manager and/or buyer, you should perform as if it were full. Do one or two of your best "talk spots," particularly if they are humorous and show your ability to relate to the audience. Don't rush through your audition, even if you feel awkward performing for only one or two people. But keep your "audition set" tight; move quickly from one song to the next and try to finish with a bang. Remember that you're selling yourself. This is your opportunity to prove you're as good as you say you are.

Wherever possible, ask the club manager or entertainment buyer to let you audition when there are people in the club, in other words, during regular hours. This is by far preferable to playing to an empty room. In many cases, if you ask, you can do what is called a "guest set" while the main act is on a break. Or if the club has a "new talent night," ask to be included. This way, at least you will have an audience to sing for and the chances of your getting a good reaction and a job are vastly improved.

Now that you are self-contained musically and, hopefully, are working several nights a week, there are other things you must be doing. First, as discussed in the previous chapter, you should be making demos whenever you can. This is especially important once you are working, for demos are one of the best ways to develop a recording style which ultimately could lead to a national career. Also, making demos is good for morale. Working night after night in small clubs can get depressing. You begin to wonder if you're getting anywhere. Demos can be your ticket out, your passport to the top. In the recording studio, you can, indeed must, sing original or unfamiliar material. You have more freedom than you do in a club to shape your own, distinctive sound. And your musicians will be grateful for the chance to get some recording experience.

## TV EXPOSURE & "VIDEO DEMOS"

At this point in your career, you also could use a video tape of yourself performing, which brings us to the subject of doing local and syndicated television shows. While it is difficult to get on national television, it is easier to get on local TV shows which originate in your area. Call the TV stations in your city and ask which shows are produced locally. In many cities, there is an early morning variety-talk show (a local version of NBC's "Today" show or ABC's "Good Morning America"), a Saturday or Sunday afternoon community-oriented show and, frequently, a latenight, local variety-talk show. Also, there are mid-afternoon shows and local charity telethon programs in most major cities. Your appearance on local shows of this type will not lead to much more than some good, regional exposure, but you can come away with a video tape cassette which could prove very helpful in promoting yourself for other TV appearances and jobs. If you are successful at getting booked on any TV show, tell the show's producer *in advance* that you would like a video cassette of your appearance on the program. The cost of a cassette copy may be anywhere from $20 to $35, but it is well worth it. For you then will have an impressive "video demo" which you can show to entertainment buyers, agents, managers and record producers as well as other TV producers.

(Most television studios make video cassettes on 3/4" machines such as JVC. Home video recorders—Betamax, RCA and Panasonic—are 1/2" machines and, unfortunately, a 3/4" tape cannot be played on a 1/2" machine and vice versa. In most professional situations, you're better off having a 3/4" cassette but, if you can afford it, it is wise to have both sizes made.)

If you are unable to arrange an appearance on a local TV show or telethon in your area, consider the feasibility of going into a local TV studio, as you would a recording studio, and producing your own "video demo." While it is virtually impossible to estimate what this will cost in every area, it may not be as expensive as you think. In many cities, for several hundred dollars you can spend an hour in a television studio and come out with a simply produced, effective, color video presentation tape which can help you generate thousands of dollars in future bookings. Keep in mind that the impact of a video presentation is tremendous. When a buyer or agent sees you "on television," he or she is bound to be impressed.

Another way to get exposure is on the nationally syndicated variety-talk shows. "The Mike Douglas Show," "Dinah!," "The Merv Griffin Show" and "Phil Donahue" are examples of this type of show. Syndicated shows are distributed differently than programs on the networks (NBC, CBS and ABC). A network show like "The Tonight Show" on NBC airs the same day it is made (except for re-runs) on all of the network's affiliated stations around the country. A syndicated show like "Dinah!" typically airs three or four weeks after it is made and then only in cities where her show has been sold, often on different days and at differing times in each city. Whereas "The Tonight Show" is guaranteed distribution to a certain "network audience" (everyone watching NBC at 11:30 pm or 10:30 pm Central) each night, Dinah Shore is sold to individual stations across the country and usually is seen during daytime viewing hours. Consequently, booking agents, producers and other show business executives are more likely to discover you on "The Tonight Show."

Still, syndicated shows are an effective means of exposure for singers and, in most cases, they are somewhat easier to get on than network shows. If you live in Los Angeles, you're in the right place to approach nearly all of the syndicated talk shows. As this is being written, all of the talk shows except Phil Donahue, which originates from Chicago, are taped in Hollywood. If you can get on any one of them, you can be assured of getting excellent national exposure as well as an opportunity to make a "video demo."

In order to get on any TV show, however, you must give the show a reason to book you. It is not enough simply to be good at what you do. Television shows book guests who can do something for the show— either attract viewers or add substantially to the show's entertainment value. When you're a "new face," an unknown quantity, it's difficult to convince the people who book these shows to put you on. You have to have something special. You have to be the only escaped convict ever to have turned from a life of crime to a life of music. Or you have to have an unusually powerful piece of material which makes you desirable. You might do a comedy song or a routine in which you sing and swallow swords at the same time. This may sound ridiculous but the fact is a TV producer is not going to book you on his show unless you give him an angle. Remember your name and face mean nothing to the viewing audience. You have to be able to do something no one else can do; you have to have a story no one else has.

Some of the talk shows which are taped in Los Angeles periodically hold open auditions for new talent. Call these shows and ask how you can audition. Prepare two songs for the audition, but make certain they are unique. Also, be sure the songs you choose are up-tempo and suitable lyrically for television. As a rule, TV producers don't like ballads. They prefer short, lively numbers.

## EXPANDING YOUR BASE FOR JOBS

Your next task is to try to build as broad a base for jobs as possible. If you work only in clubs, restaurants and lounges, you will be exposed to only one type of audience. You need experience performing before different types of audiences, and it is highly desirable to circulate in your community and become known by its most influential members. Hence, you should try to get bookings to perform for local women's groups, civic organizations (Lions, Elks, Rotary, etc.) and private conventions. You should audition for local radio and TV commercials. You should investigate working in local musical theater productions. And you should try to get small parts in films, especially industrial films or corporate sales films which may be being made in your city.

The best way to get a job performing for women's groups and civic organizations is to come up with a program designed specifically for this type of audience, a program which is entirely different from the act you would do in other places. These groups are not interested in hearing, nor are they set up to present, a typical concert or club show. What would be far more effective and saleable would be a "theme show." For example, you might offer a program built around the songs of Barry Manilow and call it "I Write the Songs . . . The Manilow Magic." Your opening number would be a Manilow hit; your opening "talk spot" would tell the history of Manilow's rise to stardom; the body of the program could be a medley of Manilow's most familiar songs; and your closing number could be a song which appropriately restates the theme. Include humor, wherever possible, and any other elements which will help make the show a complete, entertaining experience. Another saleable theme show concept would be "The History of American Musical Theater, 1920-1970." Here again, the theme would dictate your choice of songs and what you say. "Broadway Today" is a theme which would enable you to do the best-known songs from currently popular Broadway musicals. "America As Seen Through Her Popular Music" is a theme concept which might include such songs as "Don't It Make You Wanna Go Home," "Draft Dodger Rag," "God Bless America," "Country Roads," "Rocky Mountain High," "This Land Is Your Land" and "Are You From Dixie?" You also could build theme shows around such subjects as heroes in American music, work songs of America or the history of country music.

Women's groups and civic organizations are accustomed to paying anywhere from $150 to $500 for programs of this type, depending on the reputation of the performer. And in most instances, you can perform this kind of program with minimum musical accompaniment—a pianist or guitarist would suffice—thus making it a good source of additional income as well as experience.

## ASSOCIATING WITH INFLUENTIAL PEOPLE

Throughout your career, you must work at cultivating friendships and relationships with influential people—civic leaders, business people, other performers, musicians, songwriters and producers—who can recommend you for jobs. By performing for a group of women, for example, you might come to the attention of an entertainment buyer whose wife is in the audience. If she goes home and tells her husband she thinks you're terrific and he should book you, you may get a job you would not have gotten otherwise. Associating with fellow performers and musicians is especially valuable. It is not uncommon in our business for agents or entertainment buyers to ask one performer about another. If you are favorably recommended by your peers, you will get more jobs.

As proof of the fact that associating with other performers can be instrumental in advancing your career, Lola Falana told us, "The first person to actually believe in me as a serious talent with a future was Sammy Davis, Jr." She says Davis personally "opened doors" for her, using his influence whenever he could to help her get the exposure he felt she deserved. Likewise, Wayne Newton was aided early in his career by Jack Benny, who insisted that Newton be on one of his network TV specials. And there are numerous other examples. Spending time with performers who are more successful than you are can lead not only to lasting friendships but also to significant, new career opportunities.

## PRESS KITS & PROMOTIONAL MATERIALS

You also must invest in some basic promotional tools which will enable you to better sell yourself as well as help others sell you. Publicity pictures are one such tool. The best publicity pictures are good quality photographs of you *performing.* Given the choice, performance shots always are more effective than posed, stilted-looking studio pictures. These pictures will be the beginning of your press kit. In its simplest form, a press kit is an attractive folder which holds not only your publicity pictures, but also other promotional materials such as a biography and reprints of favorable reviews you have received.

Once you are working, you may find it useful to have postcards or "table tents" (a two-sided card folded in half which stands on a table) printed for distribution to patrons. These can have a picture of you on them and serve as an inexpensive souvenir for your "fans." Postcards also can be used to inform "fans" of up-coming engagements.

It is not necessary—in fact, most say it is "tacky"—for singers to have business cards printed. And personalized stationery certainly is optional. If you feel the need to use it, keep it simple. (If your letterhead has your address on it and you move, don't cross out the old address and write in your new one. This only makes you appear cheap. You're better off using a plain sheet of good quality paper for your correspondence.)

More and more performers are having "logos" created for them. A "logo" is a stylized way of writing your name or the name of your group. It becomes a graphic symbol for you, and it can be used on all of your promotional materials to give them continuity in appearance. A "logo" should be legible and immediately identifiable. It also should be designed so that it can be utilized in a variety of ways. (The group Chicago has an excellent "logo".

If you wish to include a biography ("bio") in your press kit, it should be brief, informative and written without the use of gratuitous superlatives. In other words, don't use words like "sensational" or "fantastic" to describe yourself. Just give the reader the facts—some personal background information, your musical accomplishments and a brief work history. If you have reviews of your work which are favorable, you may wish to include these or use excerpts in the text of your "bio." If need be, you can have your biography written by a professional writer for between $50 and $150.

## AGENTS & MANAGERS

Now, you're ready to get an agent.

Start by asking other performers to recommend agents. Then, ask club owners, managers and entertainment buyers for the names of the agencies they deal with, and ask them to recommend one or two. In most major cities, there usually are a handful of established agencies who handle a majority of the bookings in small rooms. (If necessary, look in the Yellow Pages under "Artists Managers" or "Theatrical Agents.") Contact several agents, tell them you are working and need representation, and invite them in to see one of your shows. Psychologically, it always is to your advantage to be working when you are "shopping" for agency representation. If you are between jobs, call several agents and ask each one for a 15-minute appointment in the office. Tell the agent (or secretary) where you have been working. If the agent is too busy to see you, make arrangements to drop off one of your press kits along with a tape (no more than three songs) and/or your "video demo." If you don't get a response from an agent in about a week or 10 days, go collect your press kit and demos and try another agency.

We should digress here and discuss the difference between agents (also called artists' managers) and personal managers. Agents are licensed to seek and secure employment for singers, musicians, writers, etc. Personal managers, who are not licensed, are *prohibited* from seeking or promising to seek or secure employment. An agent's job is to find work. A personal manager's job is to counsel, advise, and direct a performer in all aspects of his or her career. The agent brings you the job offer; the manager advises you on whether to accept the offer.

In actual practice, of course, this legal division of responsibilities tends to break down. Most good personal managers get involved in seeking and securing work for their clients, even though they technically are not supposed to. And many agents, particularly those who represent actors who typically do not have managers, function as advisers and counselors to their clients. The intent of the law, experts agree, is to protect the artist-performer by separating what theoretically are two different functions—securing employment and directing a career.

Under current laws, agents are prohibited from collecting more than a 10% commission on the work they secure for a client. Hence, if an agent gets you a job for $1,000 a week, that agent is entitled to a commission of no more than 10% of the gross amount, or $100 a week, so long as the job lasts. Managers, because they ostensibly are advisers and career directors, are allowed to charge whatever they wish in the way of commissions. Rumor has it that Elvis Presley was paying his personal manager, Colonel Parker, 50% commissions on his gross earnings in all areas—films, television, records, personal appearances and merchandizing. However, most personal managers work on a 15% of gross commission. So, if your agent gets you a job for $1,000 a week and your manager advises you to take it (or you take it anyway), you will pay your agent $100, or 10%, and your manager $150, or 15%. If you have both, 25% of your gross earnings comes off the top to pay them *before* you begin to pay your expenses and taxes. We discuss the financial aspects of being a singing entertainer in greater detail in the next chapter.

The reason you need an agent is two-fold: An agent can sell you more effectively than you can sell yourself, and an agent can get you jobs that you can't get for yourself. If your agent keeps you working, he or she is well worth the 10% commission you're paying. In the early stages of your career, it isn't as crucial to have a personal manager as it is to have an agent. But later on, especially if you hope to make a recording deal and pursue a national career, having a manager is essential. And again, if your manager gives you needed direction and advances your career in ways that you could not, he or she is worth every penny you pay in commissions.

In the beginning, though, what you need is a small, aggressive agency working for you. You don't need the clout of the William Morris Agency, International Creative Management (ICM) or the other large agencies located in Los Angeles and New York when you first are starting out. You need a person with better contacts than you have selling you. You need someone who believes in you, respects you and, most importantly, wants to work hard for you. When you find such a person, put the job of selling yourself in his or her hands. This will leave you with more time to devote to the important creative aspects of your career.

There are several other points to keep in mind when you are dealing with agents:

1. *Never pay an agent in advance to represent you.* Agents work on commissions. If they get you work, then you pay them.

2. *Always conduct yourself in a professional manner.* Remember that an agent puts his name and reputation on the line every time he books you. You have a responsibility both to your agent and your employer to show up for work on time and perform according to the provisions of your contract. If you get a reputation for being unreliable or unprofessional, it will affect not only your ability to find work but also your ability to find someone who will represent you.

3. *Don't take your agent for granted.* Agents are people, too. They tend to work harder for clients they like and are excited about and, therefore, you constantly must work at improving your act in order to keep your agent interested.

4. *Don't be afraid to sign with an agent.* If an agent wants to sign you to an exclusive agency representation contract, just be sure there is a release clause in the contract in the event that the agent fails to find you work. Most agency contracts contain a standard clause which states that, if the agent fails to secure employment for you for a certain period of time (usually 30 days), you may give notice of termination. You then are free to seek other representation.

5. *Don't be afraid to change agents.* This happens all the time. An agent may work hard for you for awhile then, for some reason, cease to be effective on your behalf. If this happens, discuss the situation with your agent. Say that you are unhappy with the relationship and that you want to find a new agent. This either will stimulate your agent to become more productive or get you a release from you contract.

## UNIONS

And now, a few words about unions. There are five unions to which performing artists may belong. They are: American Federation of Musicians (AF of M), American Federation of Television and Radio Artists (AFTRA), American Guild of Variety Artists (AGVA), Screen Actors Guild (SAG) and Actors Equity (Equity).

If you are working primarily as a musician, eventually you must become a member of the American Federation of Musicians (AF of M). This is the union which serves, protects and bargains for all of the professional musicians who play in symphony orchestras, musical theater productions, nightclub, opera and ballet orchestras, on television, in films, on radio and on records and tapes. Most showrooms, nightclubs and other places which hire live entertainment also are under the jurisdiction of the AF of M.

If you perform on radio or television (except if you perform only as a musician), you must become a member of the American Federation of Television and Radio Artists (AFTRA). AFTRA is one of the largest performing unions and the benefits which it provides to its members, such as pension and welfare plans and medical coverage, are among the most comprehensive available anywhere. Like most other unions, AFTRA also has a Federal Credit Union from which members in good standing can borrow money at low interest rates.

If you work primarily as a singer in nightclubs or concerts, the applicable union is the American Guild of Variety Artists (AGVA). However, in recent years, many performers have come to feel that AGVA is the least effective of all the performing unions and that, therefore, it is not essential to become a member. Also, if you are a member of the AF of M, you simply don't need to be a member of AGVA.

Membership in the Screen Actors Guild (SAG) is necessary only if you work in films, and Actors Equity is the union to which you must belong if you perform in legitimate or musical theater productions.

But it is not necessary to rush out and join all of these unions. In fact, never join a union unless you must in order to keep working. Under the Taft-Hartley Act, you are entitled to *one* job, your first, in any medium which comes under the jurisdiction of a union—nightclubs, stage, television, radio, films and recording—without having to become a union member. Of course, if you continue to work in that medium, you then must become a member of the applicable union. But once you are working, clearly it is in your best interests to be in the union anyway.

The unions overlap somewhat, so you may be wondering which ones to join. If you play an instrument on stage, you must join the AF of M. Unless you get an opportunity to perform on radio or TV, in which case you will need to join AFTRA, this is the only union to which you will have to belong. When you begin recording for a record company, you may choose to be paid either as a singer, in which case you must be in AFTRA, or as a musician in the AF of M. Join the other unions as the need arises.

## PERFORMING RIGHTS ORGANIZATIONS

There is one other membership you may need to consider. If you are a songwriter, you must affiliate either with Broadcast Music Inc. (BMI) or the American Society of Composers, Authors and Publishers (ASCAP) once someone records (and releases as a record) one of your songs or performs one of your songs on television. ASCAP and BMI are performing rights organizations. Their job is to collect the money to which you are entitled as a songwriter and/or music publisher for the use of your songs on television and radio throughout the world. Every time one of your songs is played on a radio station or performed on TV, you are entitled to a small payment called a performance royalty. BMI and ASCAP collect these royalties from the stations which use their music and make certain the payments reach their member writers and publishers. If you have your own publishing company, once one of your songs is recorded (and released) or performed on TV, your publishing company also must affiliate either with BMI or ASCAP. If you are a BMI songwriter, your songs must be published by a BMI publishing company; if you are an ASCAP writer, your songs must go into an ASCAP publishing company. (Music publishers frequently have both BMI and ASCAP affiliated companies so that they can accept and publish songs written by both BMI and ASCAP writers.) In terms of what they do and what they pay writers and publishers, BMI and ASCAP are roughly equal. Investigate both organizations for yourself and make your decision accordingly.

## PROMOTING YOURSELF

In the critical early stages of your career, the most significant achievement you can hope for is to distinguish yourself from the thousands of other singing performers who are striving for recognition. To do this, you have to be resourceful, imaginative and, at times, daring. When it comes to promoting yourself, you must leave no stone unturned. And in your search for an identity, no idea must go unexplored. Here, then, are some suggestions which, if followed or expanded upon, could help you advance your nascent career:

1. *Rotate engagements.* Don't work in one locale, lounge or restaurant too long. Determine the maximum length for a given engagement, say four weeks, then make plans to move either to another club or

lounge or to a different, nearby city. If you're doing well in one place, don't play it out by staying too long. It may be frightening at first to leave the security of an engagement which pays well for an unknown situation somewhere else. But there probably will be no other time in your career when you can afford to take such risks with so little to lose.

2. *Develop a mailing list of your fans, perhaps even a "fan club."* Ask those who come to see you to put their name and address on a list so that you can keep them informed of where you will be working. This is an inexpensive and highly effective way to take your audience with you wherever you go, within reason, of course. If the idea of a "fan club" is offensive to you, call the people who have taken an interest in your career "Friends of . . . ." Having a hard-core following of "fans" or friends can do wonders sometimes. Take the case of RSO recording artist John Stewart, for example. Stewart, formerly with The Kingston Trio, had been recording as a solo artist for several years with a number of record labels. Then, at one point in his career, he found himself between labels and unable to record the new songs he was writing. Finally, he began negotiating for a recording contract with RSO president Al Coury, but the negotiations were proceeding slowly. Coury seemed unsure of whether to sign Stewart or else other matters were distracting him. It was at this point that Stewart played an engagement at The Palomino Club in North Hollywood. As usual, John's ardent followers showed up and packed the club on opening night. From the stage, Stewart asked his audience for a favor. He asked everyone to take a post card on their way out after the show and send it to Al Coury at RSO Records, urging Coury to sign Stewart to the label. A few days later, Coury was beseiged with over 400 post cards, each one individually written. Now, you may not think 400 is a very impressive number. But any TV executive will tell you that anytime more than 20 or 30 people are motivated to write in on any one subject, heads turn and people listen. John Stewart was signed to RSO almost immediately.

3. *Develop sex appeal.* Don't cover up your sexuality for fear that it will get you in trouble. Use it. Sex appeal is a factor in selling every type of product, including singers. Of course, the best kind of sexuality

is that which flows naturally from a person. Contrived sexuality or sensuality is likely to be laughed at or, at the very least, viewed as distracting. If ever you feel someone in our business is trying to exploit you sexually, remember this: Give a person the benefit of the doubt, take a chance, but always protect yourself; never compromise yourself or your principles merely to advance your career.

4. *Move to a Major City.* Our survey of singers shows that 75% said they first began to experience some success while living and working in a big city such as New York (33%), Nashville (16%), Los Angeles, London, San Francisco or Atlanta (the other 26%). It is not impossible to become a successful singer in a small city or town, indeed you may have no other choice in the beginning. But once you become the hottest act in Sioux City, Iowa, then what do you do? Go to Des Moines? The recording, television and film business nowadays is concentrated in Los Angeles, California and its environs. Obviously, New York still is the home of many Broadway musicals, most high fashion modeling and a good deal of record and TV commercial production. Nashville remains the center for country music. But Los Angeles is the New Entertainment Mecca. While the competition may be more fierce in Hollywood, the number of opportunities to break into the "Big Time" also is greater. The sprawling Los Angeles Area is populated by more than 7 million people and includes dozens of out-lying communities where singers can work. While it is true not everyone who is talented makes it in L.A., hundreds, perhaps thousands do make it in our business because they live in the Entertainment Capitol of the World.

If you should decide to move to Los Angeles, be prepared to spend the first year getting your bearings. Find a "backer" (investor) who is willing to loan you money until you get established, or save enough of your own money to support yourself for at least six months without working. (Hopefully, it won't take you six months to find work if you look aggressively, but you will be a lot happier, not to mention more comfortable, if you bring your own financial cushion.) Make arrangements before you go, if you possibly can, with people who can help you find work or point you in the right direction once you arrive.

Again, such a move may seem frightening, especially if you are leaving a city or town in which you are somewhat established and secure. But moving to Hollywood can be rewarding. The Captain and Tennille were discovered at The Smoke House restaurant in Burbank. Elton John's career in the U.S. was launched at Doug Weston's Troubador on Santa Monica Boulevard, as were the careers of many other pop singers. Glen Campbell made a good living as a studio musician in Los Angeles for years before he was tapped to do a summer show for CBS replacing The Smothers Brothers. Paul Williams made a decent living as an actor and songwriter before he got the chance to become a recording artist in his own right. That's Hollywood—there are a million such stories there. These are just a few of them.

## GOING NATIONAL

This chapter rightfully should conclude with some talk about the realities of taking a localized singing career and turning it into one which has national, even worldwide, dimensions. Let's assume that, thanks to your musical director, your musicians, an outstanding agent or two and your own talent and resourcefulness, you now are gainfully employed as a singing entertainer. Your own small business, of which you still are the boss, has become a financially and creatively viable enterprise. You're making a more-than-comfortable living, say bringing home as much as $1,000 a week. Your agent has you working in the best lounges and nightclubs in major hotels. Your name is on the marquee out front. You have your own dressing room. In other words, you have reached the upper-most level of the hotel-restaurant-lounge circuit in your particular area of the country. This is an impressive achievement. However, outside of the area in which you work, few people know who you are. You're still a *local act* or, at best, a regional act. You're making a lot of money, but you don't have a record deal. You're headlining in the rooms you play, but you're not getting any offers to perform on television. What, then, is the status of your career?

Realistically, you are nothing more than "a big fish in a small pond," as the saying goes.

For the "big pond" is inhabited by artists ("big fish") who are making records, playing main rooms, theaters and concerts and performing on network TV, perhaps even in films. This is the level you must aspire to reach, the level at which you are being exposed to the mass audience and where there is a demand, not just for entertainment in general, but for *you* in particular. Until you become a nationally recognizable name act at this higher level, you must understand that you will be relegated to the position of "would-be star". You have made it to the first plateau of the mountain, now you must climb to the summit.

## A TEAM FOR SUCCESS

In order to make the ascent to the top, you need a personal manager. You need someone on your side who has a good "track record" in the business, that is, someone who has been to the top before. You need a manager who knows agents, record producers, TV and film producers and has entrée to the major record companies, the TV networks and motion picture studios. You need a manager who can help you get national exposure.

When it comes to breaking-out nationally, the role of the personal manager never has been more important. Record companies, for example, don't sign singers so much as they sign *packages*—a combination of the right singer with the right producer, the right manager, the right agency representation, the right public relations outfit and so on. The reality is that it takes a team of experienced, creative, professional people to launch a national career. Thus, the moment you become self-sufficient as a singing entertainer, and before you become too comfortable with your success at the nightclub/lounge level, you must begin to think about how you are going to assemble such a team to guide your career to the very highest levels.

Finding a personal manager may take some time. As with finding an agent, the best way to start is by asking fellow performers for recommendations. Without question, the most successful and most powerful managers are headquartered in Los Angeles, Nashville and New York. The qualities you should look for in a manager are, first, a strong interest in your career. Next, you must try to assess whether a manager is honest and has the knowledge, ability and time required to produce results for you. Finally, you should try to determine whether a manager has the power to get things done—does he have clout?

Your relationship with your manager should be as close as any you ever will have in business. You must involve him or her creatively in your career. You must trust his or her judgment and follow the advice you are given. (If you find yourself consistently disagreeing with your manager, find a new one.) And you must keep growing artistically in order to keep your manager excited about your career.

The first time you meet a manager who flatters you with statements like, "You could be a superstar" or "You've really got what it takes to make it," you may be tempted to turn over your small business to him, even make him Chairman of the Board. And he may try to convince you that the only way he can work with you is by taking over. Keep in mind, however, that you pay a manager a sizeable part of your income to work for you. You are not working for him. You hire a manager to personally represent you, to make creative suggestions and to be a consultant to your "small business." But *you* must remain Chairman of the Board. Where possible, sign a year-to-year contract with your manager. Make him prove himself to you, and never pay him more than 15% of your gross income. Also, remember that your agent should keep you working, but your manager is responsible for the advancement of your career. If he is not moving your career forward on a day-to-day basis, you don't need him.

Many performers are under the mistaken impression that powerful managers (and agents) *make* "stars." There is no real evidence to support this theory. To the contrary, Jerry Weintraub, currently one of the most prominent and successful manager-producers in the music business—his clients include John Denver, Neil Diamond, Bob Dylan,

# ILLUSTRATION: CHAIRMAN OF THE BOARD

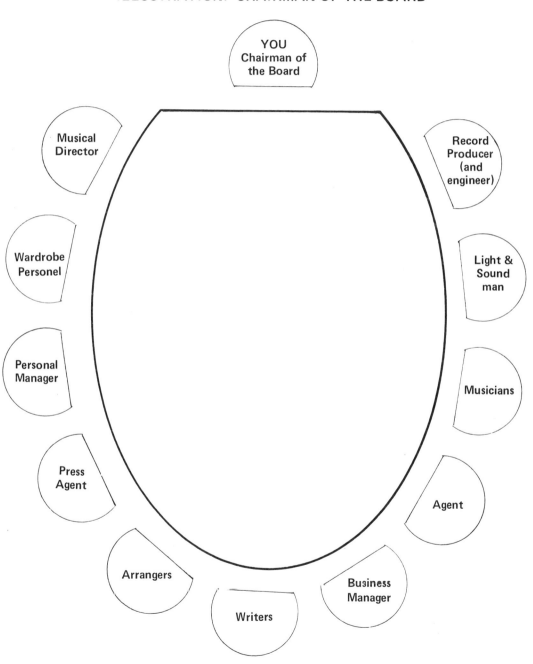

John Davidson, Roger Miller, Dorothy Hamill, The Carpenters, Bobby Goldsboro, The Pointer Sisters, Harry Chapin and The Moody Blues— says success is the result of talent, *not* management.

"All the artists that I work with, that anybody works with, get their own careers going," Weintraub told an interviewer from *Talent & Booking* magazine. "The artists who become successful are talented people. And they either write a song that the public accepts or they make a film or they do a television show that the public accepts . . . it's my job to bring it to the attention of the public and merchandize it and sell it. But it's their talent that makes them stars. I don't make stars. I'm not a kingmaker or a starmaker or any of those things that I've been labeled. The artists, in fact, are in charge of their own destinies. It's very difficult to make a star. What you can do is make sure that they get paid properly, make the decisions along with them—I don't make any decisions myself, they're all made along with the artist. I can suggest things, I can offer counsel, I can advise them, I can promote their careers . . . that's what I do. I don't make stars," he concludes.

Nevertheless, in successful music careers, personal managers are indispensible. And your search for the right manager, however long, will be worth it when you find the individual who can help you move your career out of the backwaters where you must begin and into the mainstream where you want to be.

CHAPTER 10

# MAKING MONEY

*"Honey, I've been rich and I've been poor. And* rich *is better."*
        *—Pearl Bailey*

**The entertainment business** is the only business in which, when you ask someone how much money he made last year, he tells you his *gross*. In any other industry, if you ask someone how much he made last year, he will tell you his *net*.

Performers especially are guilty of this, either because they enjoy leaving the impression that they're doing better than they really are, or because they don't fully understand the financial realities of their own business.

The purpose of this chapter, therefore, is to tell you some of the cold, hard, financial facts of life in the entertainment business. If you want to mislead others or yourself about how much you are making, that's your prerogative. But if you want to make money as a singing entertainer and, in the end, have something to show for all your hard work, you must pay close attention to financial matters as well as creative.

## YOUR GROSS

Your gross income is the sum total of all the money you take in from all sources. The five primary sources of income for singers are: personal appearances, recording, songwriting-music publishing, television and films. Some singers also earn money by writing books, performing in legitimate or musical theater productions, appearing in radio or TV commercials and, in a few cases, by merchandizing products such as lunch boxes, tee-shirts, souvenir programs, posters, games and toys.

At the start, most of your income will come from personal appearances, in other words, from the restaurants and lounges where you perform. As your career progresses, however, your income from personal appearances may grow to include fees from such lucrative venues as Las Vegas, Reno-Lake Tahoe, concerts, state fairs and tent theaters. Headliners in the main rooms in Las Vegas' glittering casino-hotels can make $100,000 or more a week. Performers who have had a couple of hit records can make anywhere from $10,000 to $50,000 per night and more in concert (so-called "one-nighters"). State fairs often pay major, name performers as much as $50,000 for one or two shows, sometimes more.

If you secure a recording deal, you then may have income from the sale of your records (called artist's royalties). However, just because you may be fortunate enough to be making records does not mean you will earn artist's royalties right away. First, you have to sell enough records to repay the record company for the costs of signing you (i.e., advances against royalties which you receive as an inducement to sign) and making your records (i.e., all recording costs, including studio time, musicians, tape, cartage, producer's fees, etc.). And only after the company has recouped these costs, which, incidentally, are agreed upon in advance and spelled out in your contract, will you begin to earn any royalties from recording. Still, making records—even if you're not earning royalties—usually has a positive effect on your income in other areas. There's more demand for your personal appearances (concert tours, in turn, help sell records), you get bigger fees and, as a recording artist, you are more sought-after by television shows. With or without a record deal, songwriting and music publishing can be a considerable source of income for singers who write and publish their own songs. Since songwriters and publishers earn money from each record sold (called mechanical royalties), it is possible to make money both by recording your own songs and by having them recorded by others. In addition to mechanical royalties earned from the sale of records, singer-songwriters also earn performance royalties, as we have seen, from BMI or ASCAP for the use of their songs on radio and television. The writer of a hit song, depending on how many records are sold and how often it is performed on radio and TV, can earn as much as $40,000 to $50,000 in mechanical and performance royalties. If the writer also is the one who has recorded the hit, then he also may earn a substantial amount in artist's royalties from the record company. Clearly, the financial rewards of being both a singer and songwriter can be immense.

Nor is it necessary to publish your own songs in order to do well as a songwriter. Writing, by itself, can be very profitable. Let's say, for instance, that you are able to land a job as a staff songwriter for a music publisher, which means you give up the publishing interest (copyright ownership) in your songs. In order to hold you exclusively to his company, the publisher must pay you a minimum of $6,000 a year. This money is, in effect, an advance against future royalties you may earn as a writer. (In deals of this kind, even though you have "sold" your songs to a publisher, you do *not* give up your writer's royalties.) If one of your songs becomes a hit, either by you or by someone else, the publisher first recoups what he has paid you to be on staff (the advances against your writer's royalties), then pays you whatever additional amounts to which you may be entitled. A million-selling record would earn on the order of $10,000 in mechanical royalties for the writer, not including performance royalties from BMI or ASCAP.

Thus, if you've been with your publisher for only one year and have received only $6,000 in advances, you can expect to receive an additional $4,000 in writer's royalty payments for your hit song. Needless to say, songwriting can pay a lot of bills.

Television appearances are another potential source of income for singers. Big-name stars can command as much as $30,000 for a single appearance on a prime-time, network variety TV special. The variety-talk shows ("The Tonight Show," "Merv," etc.) pay AFTRA scale, which only amounts to three or four hundred dollars. But appearances on such shows help performers bolster their income in other areas—television helps sell books, records and personal appearances. If you ever should be so lucky as to get your own variety or situation comedy series on television, you may find yourself earning as much as $20,000 or $30,000 a week, perhaps much more, just from television. When you calculate what this kind of exposure does to increase your income in other areas—personal appearances and recording, for example—you begin to understand why weekly television is financially so desirable. Instead of just earning dollars, you may be earning "mega-dollars."

Feature films, TV and radio commercials, books, legitimate and musical theater and merchandizing can generate still more income for singing entertainers. Typically, however, even if you are a superstar, your income from these activities, while considerable, is likely to be less predictable. Some singing entertainers, such as Sinatra, Dean Martin, Bing Crosby and Elvis, have had prolific and profitable acting careers in motion pictures, but many others have not. Likewise, some singers are fortunate in getting contracts for radio and TV commercials, others are not. Shaun Cassidy, because he is both a TV and recording star and teen idol, is capable of earning considerable sums through the merchandizing of such products as lunch boxes and posters. But the majority of singing entertainers do not have an opportunity to earn income in this way. How much a singer makes, after all, is a factor not only of individual talent, but also of public acceptance.

## YOUR NET

Where most singers get into trouble financially is in forgetting that, as in any business, there are substantial expenses involved in being an entertainer. You can't live on your *gross* income or you will be living far beyond your means. Your life style must reflect your actual, *spendable* yearly income—what you have left after operating expenses and taxes. This is called your *net*. And if you don't pay attention to your expenses and carefully manage your out-flow of money, as well as your income, you may find yourself working like the daring, high-wire circus performer—without a net. In other words, you'll have no financial cushion beneath you at all.

As we have seen, if you have both a personal manager and an agent working for you, you will have to pay out a total of 25% of your gross earnings in commissions, before you take care of any other expenses. If you're making $100,000 a year (all of which is commissionable by both agent and personal manager), this leaves you with $75,000 after commissions. Now, you must pay arrangers, musicians, travel expenses and per diem payments for hotels and food. And then you may have numerous other things to pay for—sets, a sound system, wardrobe, technical personnel (lighting and sound), office expenses (telephone, a secretary, postage, xerox copying, etc.), business management and public relations. Business managers, who manage your financial affairs, handle your payroll, pay bills and prepare your tax returns, typically work on a 5% commission basis, and the other expenses combined generally amount to 30% of the gross. So, here is what is happening to your gross income:

10% goes to your agent
15% goes to your manager
 5% goes to your business manager
30% goes to pay all of your other expenses, including musicians
    salaries, arrangers, travel, per diems, equipment, wardrobe,
    technical personnel, a PR company, office expenses, legal
    fees, etc.

Suddenly, 60% of your gross earnings is gone. It hasn't just disappeared. It has gone to pay the legitimate, customary costs of operating your business. You are doing well if you can net, *before* federal and state income taxes, 40-50% of your gross. Which means if you're making $100,000 a year, $55,000 to $60,000 will come off the top for expenses, leaving you with only $40,000 to $45,000 before Uncle Sam steps in. Let's say you and your business manager are masters at cost-cutting, though, and somehow you manage to trim your expenses to $50,000. This leaves you with $50,000 before taxes. After state and federal income taxes, your net, spendable income for the year is approximately $33,000—one-third of your gross income. And you thought you were making $100,000 a year?

## HOW TO SAVE MONEY

What can you do to hedge against the inevitable shrinkage of your gross?

When you start earning between $70,000 and $100,000 per year gross ($40,000 to $50,000 taxable), form a corporation. Once you are incorporated, your company provides your services as a singer, songwriter, recording artist, performer and so on to whomever wishes to buy (hire) these services. This is known as a "personal services company." All payments are made to your corporation, which in turn pays you a salary and makes disbursements to cover your expenses. The biggest advantage to being incorporated is that your corporation now can establish a pension and profit sharing plan for your eventual benefit. But you don't have to pay income taxes on the money you pour into your pension and profit sharing plan until you actually receive the money. The idea is to shield part of your income from taxes (you're in a tax bracket, remember) at a time when you least need it, and then take the money out at a time when your income is lower and you are in a lower bracket.

Keep track of your expenses. All of the expenses you incur in the course of doing business as an entertainer are deductible for income tax purposes in the year in which you incur them. Which means, almost everything is deductible—musicians and arranger's salaries, charts, travel expenses, going to movies, buying records, stereo equipment, instruments, TV sets, even subscribing to cable TV. Of course, commissions paid to managers and agents, as well as fees (or commissions) paid to business managers and attorneys, also are deductible. Most wardrobe is *not* deductible, even though it may be clothing you wear as part of your profession. If your stage clothes are the type of clothing also worn for personal use, their cost is not deductible. Uniforms are deductible, as are costumes which would not be worn in public as personal clothing.

If you're planning on getting married strictly to save on your taxes, don't bother. The tax rate for single taxpayers is slightly higher than for married taxpayers, but not enough to justify getting married. On $46,000 taxable income, the federal tax for a single person would be approximately $17,000; the federal tax if you were married would be approximately $14,000. The federal tax rate on earned income over about $47,000 is 50% whether you're married or single.

If you are a reasonably organized type of person who is capable of doing some light bookkeeping, you can save yourself the expense of a business manager until such time as you decide to incorporate. Keep track of your income, save your receipts for expenses, and when tax time rolls around, take everything to an accountant who understands the entertainment business. The accountant will prepare your tax returns and advise you on how to enjoy even greater savings, all for a flat fee or an hourly charge. The savings here is considerable. If you're grossing $50,000 a year, a business manager on a 5% commission would be taking $2,500. An accountant, on the other hand, probably will charge you between $150 and $500, depending on how much time he spends, for doing the same thing a business manager would do.

## BUSINESS MANAGERS & ATTORNEYS

When your income reaches the $70,000 to $100,000 level, however, and you want to incorporate, you need a business manager. Customarily, business managers will provide a complete financial service for 5% of your gross income. This service should include paying bills, handling payroll for musicians and other personnel, banking, budgeting and tax return preparation. A good business manager also will give you investment advice or help you arrange financing, if you need it. Once your income reaches a certain level, you should arrange to pay your business manager on a flat-fee basis. For example, if you're making $500,000 a year gross, and will be paying your business manager $25,000 a year for essentially the same services he was providing when you made $250,000 a year and he made $12,500. Your income has doubled, but his job hasn't become twice as difficult. So, the $500,000 a year level is a good, though perhaps somewhat arbitrary, cutting off place in terms of your business manager. At that point, switch to a flat fee of $25,000 a year and, if your business manager is fair-minded, he will be satisfied with your new arrangement.

Never pay a lawyer on a commission basis. Attorneys should work for a flat fee or on an hourly basis, not on a percentage. The main reason for this is that, once a lawyer has reviewed a contract or drafted an agreement on your behalf, the job is done. He or she is not going to be involved in the day-to-day business of running your career. Percentage deals should be reserved for those people who are intimately involved in advancing or guiding your career day in and day out—your agent, your personal manager and, to a point, your business manager.

It is wise, also, to insist that those who assist you in your career maintain separate functions. Your personal manager should be independent from your agent; your business manager should operate independently of both your personal manager and your agent; and your attorney should be an objective fourth party. While it is desirable for each entity to cooperate with the other, it is dangerous for them to become too interrelated. For if they do, there will be no one to whom you can turn if you are dissatisfied with the results you are getting in any one area.

## CONTRACTS

Although you may find it distasteful personally or think it unnecessary, it is essential that all agreements be put in writing. The entertainment business, like every other business, runs best when each party knows what is expected of him. Take the time to read and understand the provisions of any agreement you are asked to sign. If you have questions or wish to make changes, consult your attorney, agent or manager. Too many performers adopt the attitude that they should not concern themselves with contracts. This is ridiculous. From the moment you accept your first job, your life will be governed by one sort of contract or another, verbal or written. You might as well accept this fact and, if you can, use it to your advantage.

Once you have an agent and, later, a manager, you won't be required to do much more than sign contracts. Even so, always be sure you know what you're signing. When you are starting out, use the standard AF of M contract forms for your engagements. Most of the time, the restaurant or lounge manager or entertainment buyer will provide you with a contract. It's not a bad idea, though, to pay a visit to your local AF of M office and pick up a few blank contracts. Familiarize yourself with the procedure for filling out the contract form and filing it with the Union. This way, if a club manager or buyer fails to produce a contract for your "gig" (engagement), you can.

If you are working in a non-union situation, or if the form contract is not suitable, a simple contract (see appendix) or an agreement written in the form of a letter from one party to another will suffice. Simply state the deal as you understand it—*who* the employer is, *what* the job is, *when* the job is to be performed (include working hours), *where* the job is to be done, and *how much* you are to be paid. (It also is advisable to stipulate when payment is to be made and in what form, i.e., in cash or by certified check.) When signed by you and your employer, a letter agreement of this type, sometimes referred to as a "deal memo," offers you greater legal protection than a mere verbal agreement.

Whatever the agreement is and whatever it's purpose, always put it in writing (or have the other party put it in writing). This is especially important when you are dealing with friends or people you know. Never feel embarrassed to ask for a contract. Remember that everyone respects a prudent business person. Part of being a professional is knowing how to use and using professional business tools.

Here are some other points which apply to contracts and negotiating:

1. If you have special requirements in order to present your âct, these should be spelled out clearly in an attachment called a "Rider Agreement." The purpose of a Rider is to inform the employer in advance of what he must provide so that you can do your show. Riders frequently include such requirements as the size of the stage, the number of elevated platforms needed, the specifications for the sound system and stage lighting, the number of dressing rooms needed and so on (see appendix).

2. By and large, it is better to sign short-term contracts, particularly when you are beginning. Your price has nowhere to go but up, so don't lock yourself into a long-term contract at a low price.

3. Where possible, try to structure contracts for engagements so that you receive a fee for performing *plus* a separate sum for expenses. Only the fee for your performance should be commissionable by your agent or manager. Whatever you receive for expenses, say for travel, musicians, equipment, accomodations, etc., should not be commissionable. After all, this is money which simply is passing through your hands.

4. Remember that a good deal is a deal which is good for *both* parties.

5. No one can *force* you to perform. If you find yourself in an intolerable contractual jam, you have the right to refuse to perform. Of course, you must be prepared to suffer the consequences. You may be sued. But, when it comes down to it, no one can make a singer sing, an actor act or a dancer dance. Sometimes, you have to threaten, as we say, to "take that big show business walk," that is, withhold your services, in order to get what you want and deserve.

One final thought: When in doubt on any legal or financial matter, *buy* the best professional advice you can afford. Consult an attorney or a Certified Public Accountant (CPA).

# CHAPTER 11

# STRETCHING AS YOU GROW

*"All of your dreams came true/
Still, it's not enough for you/
You feel disillusioned down inside/
That's how it is with dreams/
When you have arrived it seems/
The best part of the journey is the ride"*
— *"Didn't You Always Dream
of Livin' In Malibu?" by Cort
Casady © 1978 Al Gallico Music
Corp. Used with permission.*

**There is no end to the work** of being a successful singing entertainer.

There is no end to the search for new and entertaining material.

There is no end to the need to improve and extend your talents.

There is an end to this book, however, as there must be. The temptation is to go on forever trying to cover every conceivable point and pass along every conceivable piece of good advice. But it is appropriate to begin our conclusion by going back to the basic goals set forth early in the book. You want to be able to entertain people in a life-long career. You want to become a total performer. You want to be respected by all types of audiences—young and old, rich and poor, "hip" and "square," urban and rural. You want to become "an original," not a copy. And you want to be a "class act."

Try never to lose sight of these far-reaching goals.

Don't cop out by saying, "Oh, this is okay for Peoria because they don't know any better." *You* know better.

Don't resort to cheap tricks or tasteless material just because it'll get a laugh. Your audience deserves the best you can offer.

221

Your opinion of yourself reflects your opinion of your audience. If you feel and behave like a second-rate act, they will feel like a second-rate audience. Always strive for excellence. Don't settle for expedience. Keep trying for the brass ring.

Every career is bound to have its peaks, valleys and plateaus. But plateaus are the most dangerous, for they indicate stagnation. In show business, you always must try to stay in motion and build forward momentum. If you fail to keep changing and evolving, the public will leave you behind.

Whatever the status of your career, make an effort to be objective and realistic about your strengths and weaknesses—your value—as an entertainer at all times. Treat everyone with respect on your way up. You never know whose help you'll need when you're down.

Don't ever allow yourself to become a petty person who insists on measuring the size of his billing on a marquee or insists on closing a show when it doesn't matter. You can't demand respect, you must earn it.

Keep friends in perspective. Some will turn out to be "Good Time Charlies," fair weather friends who hang around when you're doing well, then suddenly disappear when you're not. Some of your friends may have difficulty accepting you as you change and progress. They unconsciously always will think of you in terms of who you were when you first met, and they will have trouble seeing you as anything else. Never allow your friends to dictate who or what you are or limit who or what you may become. Only you and, perhaps, one or two people close to you can have an accurate vision of what you are and someday will be. And remember that some of your friends may feel threatened by your career and be fearful it will affect their relationship with you. Consequently, they subconsciously may attempt to do things to keep you from succeeding. Don't allow this to happen.

If there is one serious drawback to being your own boss, as opposed to being an employee, it is that you must set your own goals and standards. If you work for someone else and do what is expected of you, you will be successful. A singing entertainer, however, is an entrepreneur. And triumph in any entrepreneurial activity requires setting realistic goals, self-motivation and self-discipline. You constantly must create new challenges for yourself. Once you have experienced some measure of success, you must be the one who says, "I'm not satisfied. I can do better." You alone must define what constitutes "success" for you and, in order to achieve that success, you must be a self-starter.

Create a new act every two years. At least give your show an overhaul. Retain your "hits," the material which is your trademark—in other words, keep your identity—but change a minimum of fifty percent of your show. There is no better tonic for a performer than a transfusion of new material. Remember that part of what you're selling is excitement. Protect your energy. Renew your commitment. Nourish your love for what you do.

From time to time, force yourself to stretch creatively. For example, you may start out playing an instrument, say piano or guitar, when you sing, and you may become adept and comfortable singing and playing simultaneously. Still, you must experiment with singing without an instrument. This will free your hands and your mind and may enable you to get more deeply involved vocally and visually in a song. It also will make you appear to be a more versatile performer. No one should have to tell you to do this. You must take the initiative.

Use reviews of your performances to learn how you can become a better performer. Examine specific criticisms and ask yourself if they have merit. If you repeatedly receive generally negative criticism, ask yourself why. Bad reviews may have some validity.

Reviews can be misleading, also. Glowing, rave reviews may be meaningless. Devastatingly bad reviews may be unfounded. Before you read any review, try to find out something about the reviewer's background, experience and general inclinations. A reviewer who knows and likes you will try to write favorably about you. Keep these reviews in proper perspective. A reviewer who hates you and your type of music will try to tear you to pieces. In the end, you mustn't rely on reviews. You must rely on audience reaction and public acceptance. There is no percentage in performing solely for reviewers, for the final verdict comes from the people.

For many entertainers, fear of *success* is as real and powerful as the fear of failure. Certainly, it is more insidious. But fearing success is normal. After all, success brings with it awesome, new responsibilities. Once you're successful, you must live up to all that you are supposed to be. Once you make it, you're competing with yourself. If you make one million-selling record, you then must try to make another one. The prospect is frightening. And there always is the specter that, even though you've attained your goals, you still will feel unfulfilled—your moment of glory won't seem glorious enough. So, as you go along, explore your feelings about success and failure. Don't be afraid to admit you have these feelings. Notice the things you unconsciously do in various situations to arrange either to succeed or fail.

It is possible to conduct your career in such a way as to maximize winning and minimize losing. Say you're living and working as a lounge singer in Houston, Texas. You're not very well known, but you feel the need to do something positive to move your career forward another step. If you rent the Houston Astrodome and try to present yourself in concert there, you're setting yourself up for a major financial disaster and professional embarrassment. On the other hand, if you rent a small theater (say 300 seats) and dilligently promote a "showcase" for your talents amongst your friends, you might do very well indeed. The former would be an effort destined to fail, while the latter would be a bold move calculated to succeed. You can arrange it either way. If you have an important audition at ten o'clock in the morning, stay up all night partying and then oversleep, missing the audition, you have arranged a loss in your career. You could have gone to bed early, or you could have scheduled the audition for later in the day. If you put your mind to it, you can plan your career so that you win at every step along the way. If necessary, take *smaller* steps so that your chances for success are greater with each one. It is essential in an endeavor where self-confidence plays such an important part to allow yourself the satisfaction of experiencing victory.

It also is axiomatic to permit those you work with to win. Some performers have the attitude that, in order to feel superior, they must make everyone else feel inferior. The flaw in this kind of thinking should be apparent. If you wish to have the aura of a winner, you must surround yourself with winners. Beware of your self-destructive tendencies, too. Most of us are afraid to be all that we possibly can be. Hence, we abuse ourselves. We drink or smoke too much or take drugs. We gain weight, which makes us less attractive, or we don't eat properly, which can lead to malnutrition, loss of vitality and even illness. Or we drive ourselves too hard. Avoid these pitfalls.

Remember that entertaining is your business, not your whole life. While you are building your professional life, you also must make sure you build a meaningful and fulfilling personal life. They go hand in hand. If you don't have both, you never will be completely happy, no matter how successful you become.

Show business is an endurance contest. Good health, physical and emotional, is essential if you hope to stay in the running. You must build up both physical and emotional stamina. And the ups and downs are inevitable, so you must develop resiliency.

In any business, no matter what its nature, it takes awhile to reach the top. Thus, you must pace yourself for the long haul. If you persist, if you dedicate yourself and if you don't burn yourself out, eventually you will be rewarded. Look around you, particularly in show business, and you will see this is true. Success comes to those who have spent the time and energy working for it.

Besides, the going should be as rewarding as the arrival. The thrilling thing about pursuing a career in show business is the sense of fulfillment you can get every day by working on some aspect of your art and craft. Though it may be hard to believe when you're living them, the "hungry years" are the best years of your life. You will look back on them with fondness, for the best part of any journey is the ride.

# SUGGESTED READING

AFTER-DINNER LAUGHTER, Sylvia L. Boehm, New York, Sterling, 1977.

AIN'T GOD GOOD, Jerry Clower, Key Word Books, 1977.

ALL THE YEARS OF AMERICAN POPULAR MUSIC, David Ewen, Englewood Cliffs, New Jersey, Prentice Hall, 1977.

AMERICAN POPULARS SONGS: FROM THE REVOLUTIONARY WAR TO THE PRESENT, David Ewen, New York, Random House, 1966.

THE ART OF INTERPRETATIVE SPEECH, Charles H. Woolbert, Severina E. Nelson, New York, Appleton Century Crofts, 1956.

BARRY MANILOW, Mark Bego, New York, Tempo Books, 1977.

BEL CANTO, Cornelius L. Reid, New York, Coleman Press, 1950.

THE BEST JOKES OF ALL TIME AND HOW TO TELL THEM, George Q. Lewis and Mark Wachs, New York, Hawthorne, 1966.

BIG STAR FALLIN' MAMA, Hettie Jones, New York, Viking, 1974.

THE BLUESMEN, Samuel Charters, London, Oak Publications, 1967.

BRAUDE'S HANDBOOK OF STORIES FOR TOASTMASTERS AND SPEAKERS, Jacob M. Braude, New York, Reward Books, 1957.

BRAUDE'S TREASURY OF WIT AND HUMOR, Jacob M. Braude, New York, Reward Books, 1964.

BREWER'S DICTIONARY OF PHRASE AND FABLE, E. Cobham Brewer, New York, Harper & Row, 1970.

THE CAROL BURNETT STORY, George Carpoz, Jr., New York, Warner Paperback Library, 1975.

COAL MINER'S DAUGHTER, Loretta Lynn, New York, Warner Books, 1976.

THE COOL FIRE: HOW TO MAKE IT IN TELEVISION, Bob Shanks, New York, Vintage Books, Random House, 1977.

THE COTTON CLUB, Jim Haskins, New York, Random House, 1977.

COUNTRY SINGERS AS I KNOW 'EM, Mae Boren Axton, Austin, Texas, Sweet Publishing Co., 1973.

COUNTRY, THE BIGGEST MUSIC IN AMERICA, Nick Tosches, New York, Stein & Day, 1977.

THE DAVID ESSEX STORY, George Tremlett.

JOHN DENVER, David Dachs, New York, Pyramid Books, 1976.

ELTON JOHN, Gerald Newman, Ontario, Signet Books, 1976.

FLIP LINES, Robert Orben, Louis Tanne, New York, 1952.

FOLK SONGS OF NORTH AMERICA, Alan Lomax, New York, Doubleday, 1960.

GAG-BONANZA, Robert Orben, Baldwin, New York, Orben Publications, 1963.

GOLDEN YEARS OF BROADCASTING, Robert Campbell, New York, Rutledge Book/Scribners, 1976.

THE GREAT AMERICAN POPULAR SINGERS, Henry Pleasants, New York, Simon & Schuster, 1967.

THE GROUCHO LETTERS — LETTERS FROM AND TO GROUCHO MARX, New York, Simon & Schuster, 1967.

HOW I WRITE SONGS — WHY YOU CAN, Tom T. Hall, Ft. Lauderdale, Florida, Ryckman & Beck, 1976.

HOW TO BECOME A PROFESSIONAL POP SINGER, Al Siegel, New York, Citadel Press, 1963.

HOW TO MAKE MONEY IN MUSIC, Herby Harris & Lucien Farrar, New York, Arco Publishing Co., 1978.

JOEY ADAMS' SPEAKER'S BIBLE OF HUMOR, Joey Adams.

JUDY GARLAND, Anne Edwards, New York, Simon & Schuster, 1975.

LET THE CHIPS FALL, Rudy Vallee, Harrisburg, Pa., Stackpole Books, 1975.

LISTEN TO THE BLUES, Bruce Cook, New York, Scribner & Sons, 1973.

LIZA, James Robert Parish, New York, Pocket Books, 1975.

MAKING IT WITH MUSIC, Kenny Rogers and Len Epand, New York, Harper & Row, 1978.

THE MAKING OF SUPERSTARS, Robert Stephen Spitz, New York, Anchor Press/Doubleday, 1978.

MERMAN, AN AUTOBIOGRAPHY, Ethel Merman, New York, Simon & Schuster, 1978.

MICK JAGGER, J. Marks, London, Abacus, 1974.

MOTOWN, David Morse, London, Rock Books, 1971.

THE MUSIC/RECORD CAREER HANDBOOK, Joseph Csida, New York, Billboard Publications, Inc., 1973.

MY HEART BELONGS, Mary Martin, New York, Warner, 1976.

MY STORY, Mike Douglas, New York, Putnam, 1978.

OFFICIAL TALENT & BOOKING DIRECTORY, Steve Tolin, Editor, Los Angeles, Tolin Publishing Co., (Annual).

ON THE ROAD WITH BOB DYLAN, Larry Sloman, New York, Bantam Books, 1978.

THE ONE AND ONLY BING, Bob Thomas, New York, Grosset & Dunlop, 1977.

THE OUTLAWS, Michael Bane, New York, Dolphin, 1978.

PULLING YOUR OWN STRINGS, Dr. Wayne Dyer, New York, Funk & Wagnalls, 1978.

RHYMING DICTIONARY, Clement Wood, Garden City, New York, Doubleday & Co., 1936.

ROCK – THE STORY OF ROCK FROM ELVIS PRESLEY TO THE ROLLING STONES, Mike Jahn, New York, Quadrangle, 1973.

ROCK ALMANAC, Charlie Gillett and Stephen Nugent, New York, Anchor Press, 1978.

ROCK ON – THE ILLUSTRATED ENCYCLOPEDIA OF ROCK N' ROLL, Norm N. Nite, New York, Crowell, 1974.

ROCK ENCYCLOPEDIA, Lillian Roxon, New York, Grosset's Library, 1971.

THE ROCKIN' 50'S, Arnold Shaw, New York, Hawthorne, 1974.

SINATRA, Earl Wilson, Scarborough Ontario, Canada, Signet Books, 1977.

SINGIN' AND SWINGIN' AND GETTIN' MERRY LIKE CHRISTMAS, Maya Angelou, New York, Random House, 1976.

SPEAKER'S BIBLE OF HUMOR, Joe Adams, Garden City, New York, Doubleday, 1972.

THE SPIDER AND THE MARIONETTES, Alan Dale, New York, Lyle Stuart, 1965.

STARS IN MY EYES, Jean Alice White, Ft. Worth, Texas, Branch Smith, 1978.

THE STARS OF COUNTRY MUSIC, Bill C. Malone and Judith McCulloh, New York, Avon, 1976.

SUCCEEDING IN THE BIG WORLD OF MUSIC, Jean & Jim Young, Boston, Little, Brown, 1977.

TAG-LINES, Robert Orben, Baldwin, New York, Orben Publications, 1954.

TAKE MY WIFE . . . PLEASE – MY LIFE & LAUGHS, Henny Youngman, New York, Putnam, 1973.

TALKING TO MYSELF, Pearl Bailey, New York, Harcourt Brace, 1971.

10,000 JOKES, TOASTS AND STORIES, Lewis & Faye Copeland, New York, Doubleday, 1965.

THIS BUSINESS OF MUSIC AND MORE ABOUT THIS BUSINESS OF MUSIC, Sidney Shemel and M. William Krasilovsky, New York, Billboard Publications Inc., 1977.

TIN PAN ALLEY, Ian Whitcomb, New York, Padding Press, 1975.

TODAY'S SOUND, Ray Coleman, New York, A Melody Maker Book, 1973.

3,500 GOOD JOKES FOR SPEAKERS, Gerald F. Lieberman, New York, Dolphin Books, 1975.

20,000 QUIPS & QUOTES, Evan Esar, Garden City, New York, Doubleday, 1968.

2,000 MORE INSULTS, Louis A. Safian, A.T.A.T., Citadel Press, 1967.

TURN IT UP, Bob Sarlin, London, Coronet Books, 1975.

VARIETY MUSIC CAVALCADE, Julius Mattfeld, Englewood Cliffs, New Jersey, Prentice Hall, 1962.

WINNERS GOT SCARS TOO – THE LIFE OF JOHNNY CASH, Christopher S. Wren, New York, Ballantine, 1971.

WHEN IT'S LAUGHTER YOU'RE AFTER, Stewart Harral, Norman, Oklahoma, University of Oklahoma Press, 1962.

THE WORLD I LIVED IN, George Jessel, Chicago, Regnery, 1975.

THE YEAR IN MUSIC – 1977, Judith Glassman, New York, Columbia House, 1977.

YES I CAN, THE STORY OF SAMMY DAVIS, JR., Sammy Davis, Jr. and Jane & Burt Boyar, New York, Farrar, Straus & Giroux, 1965.

YOUR ERRONEOUS ZONES, Dr. Wayne Dyer, New York, Avon Books, 1976.

# APPENDIX

## SAMPLE QUESTIONNAIRE

*John Davidson's*
## SINGERS' SUMMER CAMP

*Dear Larry*
*Your answers*
*would be of such*
*importance. John*

10763 WILKINS AVENUE
LOS ANGELES, CA 90024

P.O. BOX 27
AVALON, CA 90704

JD Questionnaire -1-

Questionnaire for  BARRY MANILOW

Dear Friend,

   I am in the process of writing a book about the art and business of being a singing entertainer.  The book will be published in the Spring of 1979 and, in addition to being available to the general public, it will be used by students at my annual Singers' Summer Camp on Catalina Island.

   As part of my research, I am sending this questionnaire to prominent, successful singers like yourself in hopes that you will share with me (and ultimately those who read the book) certain information about the beginnings, development and maintenance of your career.

   Please take a few minutes to complete the survey and return it to me at your earliest convenience.  By replying, you will be giving me permission to use your responses in the book.  A self-addressed, return envelope is provided.

   Writing this book is both a personal and professional challenge for me and, with your input, it will be an even more valuable tool for the many young people who aspire to do what we do.

                          Sincerely,

                          *John*

                          John Davidson

1.  Put in order of their importance (1 through 4) the qualities you think have contributed to the success of your career:
    VOCAL ABILITY ___3___
    APPEARANCE ___4___
    PERSONALITY ___1___
    PROFESSIONALISM ___2___

2.  How would you describe yourself? (check one)
    BASICALLY SHY ___X___ BASICALLY OUTGOING, GREGARIOUS _____

3.  Was music a part of your upbringing?
    YES ___X___ NO _____
    Were tjere any other musical people in your family?
    YES ___X___ NO _____

4.  Have you studied voice?  YES _____ NO ___X___
    Acting?  YES _____ NO ___X___
    Dancing?  YES _____ NO ___X___

5.  How many other singers have you seen perform live (TV dosen't count) in the last year? ___1___

6.  Which of the following do you read regularly (at least once a week):
    DAILY NEWSPAPER ___X___
    PEOPLE MAGAZINE ___X___
    BILLBOARD, CASHBOX and/or RECORD WORLD ___X___
    VARIETY and/or HOLLYWOOD REPORTER ___X___
    NEWSWEEK, TIME and/or US NEWS & WORLD REPORT ___X___

7.  Are you a college graduate?  YES _____ NO ___X___
    If yes, in what field did you receive your degree?
    _____

8.  How old were you when you first decided to pursue a career as a singer? ___26___

9.  How old were you when you first felt you had experienced some success as a singer? ___27___

10. Do you smoke?  YES _____ NO ___X___

11. Do you drink alcohol everyday?  YES _____ NO ___X___

12. Do you exercise regularly?  YES ___X___ NO _____

13. Have you ever sung with a group or a partner?  YES ___X___ NO _____
    If yes for how long? _____

14. Are you a composer or songwriter?  YES ___X___ NO _____
    If yes, how many of the songs you have written are currently in your act? ___13___

232

15. What do you do to warm up before a performance?
    VOCAL EXERCISES _____
    PHYSICAL EXERCISES _____
    BOTH VOCAL AND PHYSICAL EXERCISES _____
    MENTAL PREPARATION (including meditation) _X_____
    NONE OF THE ABOVE _____

16. When you experience vocal fatigue, do you usually lose your upper range or lower range?
    UPPER _X_____ LOWER _____

17. Can you sing two or more shows per night and still sing as well as you would like to? YES _____ NO _X_____

18. Do you sing the same way in live performances as you do when making a record? YES _____ NO _X_
    If no please explain: _Some of the tapes being what you can how___
    _____

19. Do you own a sound system (P.A.)? YES _X_____ NO _____

20. Please circle which of the following personnel are currently on your payroll:
    a. MUSICAL DIRECTOR
    b. PIANIST
    c. GUITARIST
    d. BASSIST
    e. DRUMMER
    f. ROAD MANAGER
    g. LIGHTING PERSON
    h. SOUND PERSON
    i. WARDROBE PERSON
    j. HAIR OR MAKE UP PERSON
    k. BACKGROUND SINGERS

21. Please estimate your ANNUAL expenses for the following personnel and/or services:
    MUSICIANS $ _1500_____ /yr. week
    SINGERS & DANCERS $ _____ /yr.
    WARDROBE $ _25,000____ /yr.
    SCENERY, PROPS, SPECIAL EFFECTS $ _20,000_____ /yr.
    MUSICAL ARRANGEMENTS $ _30,000____ /yr.

22. List in order of their importance to you in your career (1 thru 6):
    RECORDING _1____
    CONCERTS _2____
    NIGHTCLUBS _____
    TELEVISION _3____
    MUSICAL THEATRE _____
    FILMS _____

23. Can you read music for voice? YES _X_____ NO _____

24. To what do you attribute your first break-through as a popular singer?
    TELEVISION APPEARANCE _____
    FILM ROLE _____
    HIT RECORD _x_____
    NIGHTCLUB ENGAGEMENT _____
    BROADWAY SHOW _____
    OTHER: _____

25. In what city were you living when you were discovered or first experienced some success as a singer? _NEW YORK_____

26. Check which of the following you believe are <u>essential</u> to a successful singing career in popular music:
    ABILITY TO DANCE _____
    ABILITY TO TELL JOKES _____        *ability to be believable*
    ABILITY TO SING: Folk _____        *on stage*
                     Country _____
                     Rock'n Roll _____
                     Gospel _____
                     Jazz _____
                     Broadway _____
                     Pop _____
    ABILITY TO PLAY MUSICAL INSTRUMENTS _____
    ABILITY TO DO IMPRESSIONS _____
    ABILITY TO WRITE SONGS _____

27. Circle which of the following best describes how you usually feel when you're performing in front of an audience:
    a. I'M PLAYING A ROLE (much as an actor plays a role), portraying SOMEONE OTHER THAN MY REAL SELF.

    b. I'M BASICALLY MYSELF, BUT I ADOPT A PUBLIC POSTURE (attitude) WHEN I'M ON STAGE.

    c. ON STAGE, I FEEL I'M EXACTLY THE SAME PERSON AS I AM OFF STAGE.

28. During a typical performance, what percentage of you concentration actually is devoted to:
    a. HOW ARE YOU SINGING (your sound)............ _25_ %
    b. WHAT ARE YOU SINGING (the lyric) ........... _25_ %   *25%*
    c. WHAT THE AUDIENCE IS DOING OR THINKING...... _20_ %
    d. WHAT YOU'RE GOING TO DO NEXT................ _10_ %
    e. HOW YOU LOOK (or body movement) ............ _20_ %
                                          Total  100 %

29. In your act, how important is each of the following in terms of getting a good reaction from a typical audience. Assign a percentage to each which you think accounts for the audience reaction:
    a. MY <u>CHOICE OF MATERIAL</u> ACCOUNTS FOR _10_ % OF THE REACTION.
    b. MY <u>DELIVERY OF THE MATERIAL</u> ACCOUNTS FOR _10_ % OF THE REACTION.
    c. MY <u>ENERGY ON STAGE</u> (pacing, tempos, etc.) ACCOUNTS FOR _10_ % OF THE REACTION.
    d. MY <u>RAPPORT WITH THE AUDIENCE</u> ACCOUNTS FOR _70_ % OF THE REACTION.
                                          Total 100 %

30. Indicate which of the following people currently play an active part in maintaining and furthering your career: (1 through 9)

AGENT _____2._____

PERSONAL MANAGER ____!_____

BUSINESS MANAGER (or Accountant) ___3_____

ATTORNEY ___5_____

PERSONAL SECRETARY ___4_____

RECORD PRODUCER ___6_____

PUBLISHER ___7_____

TV PRODUCER ___8_____

Please check one:

_____✓_____You have my permission to use my name and my responses to this questionnaire in your book.

_____You have my permission to use my responses to this questionnaire in your book, but please do not use my name.

Thank you,

_____
NAME OF SINGER ..........

## SAMPLE AGREEMENT

AGREEMENT entered into this the _____ day of _____,
19___, by and between_____ (herein "Employer") and
_____, a musical group (herein "Employee").

TERMS AND LOCATION OF ENGAGEMENT: Employer hereby agrees to engage
the professional services of Employee(s), as independent contractors,
for a period of _____ (   ) consecutive days, commencing
_____, and continuing through _____
_____at the establishment known as _____
_____.

COMPENSATION: For professional services rendered as musicians, Employer
agrees to pay Employee(s) the sum of _____
_____ ($         ) for the engagement. Said payments are to
be made in cash or by certified check payable to _____
_____ upon completion of each work week.

SCHEDULED HOURS OF EMPLOYMENT: Employer and Employee(s) hereby agree
that Employee(s) shall perform _____ (   ) nights, as specified
above, from _____PM until _____AM.

SERVICES: Employee(s) agree to provide their services as professional
musicians to Employer during the times set forth herein and further
agree to conduct themselves in a professional manner at all times while
at the place of the engagement. Employer agrees that Employee(s) shall
have the sole right to determine the musical content of their performances throughout the engagement. Employer also agrees that Employee(s)
shall be entitled to three (3) fifteen minute breaks during each night
of employment.

OTHER PROVISIONS: Employer agrees to provide to Employee(s) all elements
necessary to Employee(s) performance under this agreement, specifically
a stage, stage lighting, etc.

By signing below, the parties hereto agree that the foregoing
accurately reflects the understanding between them and warrants that
each has the right or the authority to enter into this agreement.


ACCEPTED AND AGREED TO:                    ACCEPTED AND AGREED TO:

_____              _____

BY _____           BY _____

_____              _____

## SAMPLE RIDER AGREEMENT

RIDER ATTACHED TO AND MADE A PART OF AGREEMENT DATED _____
BY AND BETWEEN HIDDEN HILLS PRODUCTIONS, INC. (HEREINAFTER CALLED
"PRODUCER") AND _____ (HEREINAFTER
CALLED "PURCHASER")

_____

1. It is understood and agreed that JOHN DAVIDSON shall receive
100% Sole Star Headline billing in any and all publicity releases
and paid advertisements, including but not limited to programs,
fliers, signs, lobby boards and marquees. The form and manner of
billing and starring credits in all advertising, billboards, programs and publicity shall be determined by PRODUCER.

2. It is understood and agreed that PRODUCER may cancel the engagement hereunder by giving written notice thereof at least thirty
(30) days prior to the commencement date of the engagement hereunder
if JOHN DAVIDSON shall be called upon to render his services in
connection with theatrical motion picture (s), television, or a
legitimate stage play and if the engagement hereunder might conflict
therewith.

3. PURCHASER shall furnish PRODUCER, at PURCHASER'S sole cost and
expense, an orchestra consisting of a minimum of     musicians and
having the following instrumentation:

|  |  |
|---|---|
| 3 Trumpets | Double Flugel Horn |
| 3 Trombones | 1 Bass, 2 Tenor |
| 4 Saxophones | Alto double Flute, Piccolo, Clarinet |
|  | Alto double Tenor Saxophone, Flute, Clarinet |
|  | Tenor double Flute, Clarinet |
|  | Baritone double Bass Clarinet, Flute and Clarinet |
| 1 Fender Bass |  |
| 1 Percussion | Must play Timpani (2-3), Bells, Vibes, Tambourine, Conga, Xylophone & Bongo's. |
| 1 Electric Guitar | Doubling acoustic, banjo |

PRODUCER will supply the services of accompanist/pianist/conductor
and drummer for JOHN DAVIDSON'S accompaniment only.

- 1 -

- 2 -

It is also the responsibility and expense of the PURCHASER to furnish the following for use by the orchestra:

3a.   Grand piano (with piano bench and piano light) tuned to an A-440 International Pitch on the day of engagement and kept in tune for the duration of the engagement.  Two tunings per week are recommended, or any time piano is moved.

3b.   Identical music stands with attached lights in perfect working condition for full instrumentation.  Lights to be gelled in 825 no color pink.

3c.   The following risers:

4.  PURCHASER agrees to furnish PRODUCER, at PURCHASER'S sole cost and expense, the following for the engagement hereunder:

4a.   A first-class, low impedance, high-quality sound system consisting of a mixing console with a minimum of twenty-four (24) inputs with equalization on each input, and console is to be placed within the seating area of the place of performance.

   A high powered, high quality speaker system capable of supplying each seat in the audience with a sound pressure level (SPL) of ninety-eight decibles.

   A stage monitoring system consisting of a "woofer-horn" type speaker system capable of supplying the stage area with a SPL to overcome the audio level of the orchestra and "house" speaker system.

   Microphones, stands, cables, sub-mixers, adaptors, and accessories to adequately reproduce the vocalist and orchestra in such manner to be approved by PRODUCER.

   PRODUCER has the right to augment with PRODUCER'S own equipment and/or operate the above mentioned sound system with PRODUCER'S own personnel.

4b.   A first-class, high quality lighting system capable of lighting the performing area with a minimum of a four (4) color wash with each wash to be on its own dimmer.

- 3 -

Two carbon arc follow spotlights of the "Trouper" or "Super Trouper" types capable of being gelled in a minimum of five (5) different colors.

Cables, gells, and focusing equipment to adequately light the performing area in such manner to be approved by PRODUCER.

4c.    A stage with a performing area consisting of a minimum depth of twenty-four (24) feet, minimum width of thirty-two (32) feet and a minimum height of three (3) feet and having stairs (without hand rails) leading off the front into the audience.

Stage and place of performance should be clear of any unnecessary personnel, available and accessible to PRODUCER at least ten (10) hours prior to performance time for set-up, rehearsal and sound check. Audience and ushers are not allowed in seating area until rehearsal and sound checks have been completed and cleared with PRODUCER.

4d.    All necessary and experienced personnel in connection with the set-up and the operation of the technical equipment; the following minimum personnel must be available: two (2) men to unload equipment upon arrival and load equipment after the last performance, one (1) board man, one (1) sound man, two (2) follow spot operators, one (1) wardrobe mistress for pressing and minor repairs (iron and ironing board must be available for her use).

All personnel (except wardrobe mistress) must be available four (4) hours prior to music rehearsal.

4e.    Rehearsal (s) shall be designated as to time and length by PRODUCER. Each rehearsal shall commence at least thirty (30) minutes prior to any music rehearsal. Unless any prior arrangements have been made to the contrary, PURCHASER must provide and compensate a sound man and lighting director to PRODUCER at any and all rehearsals and shows. Minimum rehearsal time for JOHN DAVIDSON is four (4) hours.

4f.    Clear-Com brand or comparable headset intercom (subject to PRODUCER'S approval) to provide communication between stage manager, spot operators, board men and sound men.

4g.    Two (2) fully equipped star dressing rooms; one (1) large dressing room for musicians.

– 4 –

4h.   PURCHASER shall provide a locked storage area for musical instrument cases during the term of this engagement.

4i.   One (1) three (3) foot high, backless, black stool.

ACCEPTED AND AGREED TO:

HIDDEN HILLS PRODUCTIONS, INC.

_____          _____
PURCHASER                          PRODUCER

By:                                By: